Cutting Up
with Curves

For the Quilter with Limited Craft Time:

Whose view of another bed quilt is an acre of work,
Who will only undertake another project with a foreseeable
  conclusion,
Who thinks experimenting is fun,
Who displays patchwork beyond the bedroom,
Who uses visual examples to jump–start the imagination,
Who enjoys another quilter's tips, thoughts, and ideas,
Who's ready for a touch of whimsy, a pictorial or a new
  abstraction,
Who's been intending to do something with the Curved
  Two-Patch System,
This one's for you.

Cutting Up with Curves

Joyce M. Schlotzhauer

EPM
Publications, Inc.
McLean, Virginia

Other Books by JOYCE M. SCHLOTZHAUER

The Curved Two-Patch System,
A Quilter's Exciting Discovery for Creating
Pieced Flowers, Foliage and Other Patterns

Curves Unlimited,
Expanding the Curved Two-Patch System to
Soften Shapes and Create New Patterns

Library of Congress Cataloging-in-Publication Data

Schlotzhauer, Joyce M.
  Cutting up with curves.

  1. Quilting—Patterns.   I. Title.
TT835.S345   1988   746.46   88-24406
ISBN 0-939009-14-5

EPM Publications, Inc., 1003 Turkey Run Road
  McLean, VA 22101
Printed in the United States of America

Photography by Frank Borkowski
Illustrations by Sue Koval
Cover and book design by Tom Huestis

Cover photograph, **Sent With Love,** was pieced
and hand-quilted by Joyce Schlotzhauer.
From the collection of Hazel Carter.

Title page photograph, EPM logo, from a wall
hanging designed and made by Joyce Schlotzhauer
and hand-quilted by Eulalia Franzel.

Contents

Nothing from a straight line swerves
So sharply as a woman's curves,
And having swerved, no might or main
Can ever put her straight again.

SAMUEL P. HOFFENSTEIN

List of Motifs and Short Subjects

List of Photographs

The Evolving Curved Two-Patch System

SECTION ONE

*A Curved Two-Patch block
made by Janet Gillespie*

There was a time when I wasn't a quilter. I've had other interests in my life. But they are in my past. None was what you might call a true hobby. Everybody knows that hobbies have to be pursued. I was better at neglect than pursuit, so each interest fluttered briefly, languished and died. Hardly a trace remains of former pastimes, except my penchant for doodling on graph paper.

My doodling habit began in the late Sixties when my husband and I were planning to build our version of the American dream house. Waiting for the gap between our fantasies and our pocketbook to close, I whiled away a number of seasons with graph paper and pencil. I studied the concepts of architects and marveled at the talent that can create a home without clichés or geegaws from a mere functional plan. I practiced visualizing the size and shape of spaces formed by a line drawing. Trying to couple style with practicality, I drew endless room arrangements. My doodling-on-a-grid became a game. "A cheap hobby" that my husband joked about until the day we signed for a mortgage. But I like to think that all this helped me develop an observant eye.

Upon discovering quilting in the early Seventies, I found my doodling experience had been a kind of basic training in design. I reasoned that if I could design a house that hadn't collapsed and wasn't the neighborhood eyesore, I should be able to design a quilt. Of course, with the house I had a draftsman and a contractor who provided professional expertise. With quilting, I was on my own. I brought out my graph paper pads and, to the relief of my husband, began investigating the mysteries of quilt designs.

Many simple block designs, as you know, follow the straight lines of a grid. A great many more add cuts across the diagonals of a grid. Drafting becomes increasingly complex for designs based on diamonds, hexagons and other geometrics that don't fit on normal graph paper. Then there are curves, tacked onto the roster of quilt patterns like have-to-invite relatives that are eccentric and difficult.

When I became inquisitive about designing with curves, it seemed natural to use the simplest approach for diagraming patchwork: Draw each curve on the diagonal of a square grid and let the vertical and horizontal lines represent the other two edges of a curved patch. The common sense of this method revealed some advantages. Now to design quilt patterns, I could play with curves contained on a grid. What's more important, I could construct whatever I drew. (Carefully drafted templates would assure accuracy of piecing.) The more I played with this concept, the more I realized that a common-sense organization, a grid system, for simple convex and concave curves could provide quilters with an endless variety of new patterns.

A Backward Glance

Before introducing the latest phase of the Curved Two-Patch System, let me recap its development. Sometimes it helps you to see where you're being led if you know where you've been. The story began with a series of floral blocks, borders and quilt patterns. I've always thought it was a happy decision to start with flower designs. Most quilters have a built-in reluctance to try curved piecing. I can talk all I want to about curves being easy enough for anyone who isn't an absolute klutz with a needle or sewing machine; but, before straying from the customary straight lines of patches, a quilter must be inspired. I felt that floral designs would invite her down the primrose path and, at the same time, allay any fears she might have.

The original system was simple. The bias seams were technically easy because the curves were shallow and could be sewn by machine as well as by hand. This is not the case with the deeper arcs of the *Drunkard's Path*, to which I contrasted my curves. The Curved Two-Patch System was *not* a variation of the traditional pattern (although a few liked to say so). The difference was basic. With the system's arc extended completely across the diagonal of a square, curves could flow together smoothly in numerous designs without jogs interrupting the action. All the designs included concave and convex patches to be sewn into squares. The patterns evolved with the repetition and rotation of these two-patch squares, which I called units to distinguish them from the typical shape of a completed quilt block. (Remember the term *unit*. You'll see it throughout this book also.) Each design had curves of just one size to combine with other squares and rectangles. Assembly with the units aligned in rows or columns was straight-line sewing. Then to eliminate the need to draft the illustrations of the first book to full scale, I added a set of templates to trace.

So for its introduction, the Curved Two-Patch was without complications. There was a need to expand. Not all quilters want to piece designs containing only three shapes (two curves and a square). Not all quilters want to piece flowers.

During the time when I was manipulating the pair of curves into floral designs, I also toyed with substituting curves for the triangles of traditional patterns. Unique, abstract shapes transcended in the switch. With more paper trials, I found that the convex and concave patches combined to create

new-to-patchwork shapes, such as the ogee or "S" shape. I saw unusual secondary designs appear with repeated blocks of curves. According to how a design was developed, the motion of the curves could be fascinating or it could be monotonous. I realized the system had been missing the contrast of other geometric shapes. It had implied, "Curves, stick to your own kind." But too many curves without relief are. . .well, just too many. For the second book, I mixed contrasting shapes and varying sizes of curves in a series of abstract designs. Wanting other quilters to have the pleasure of personal discovery, I also added a chapter about modifying patterns and experimenting with curves. When a local guild member, Claire Benedict, told me about a better way to draw curves, I altered the drafting of the templates. These features were the basics of *Curves Unlimited*.

As I continued doodling with curves, occasionally an engaging creature would start to take shape on my graph paper. But only the simplest life forms were successful. The system's curves, for example, would neatly scallop a butterfly's wings, but who wants scallops for the long, graceful curve of a giraffe's neck?

The original curves that form a square have design limitations. A pity, because as steeped as I am in curved piecing, I've observed how full of curves our world is. And I've noticed that many quilters enjoy small projects with realistic motifs. Maybe a whimsical animal or a bit of scenery—the style of design usually meant for those who enjoy applique. Of course, it's possible to draw a design to full scale and take patterns from it. In such a freehand manner, artists and self-confident quilt designers are able to piece all sorts of odd shapes, including many types of curves. I wanted the Curved Two-Patch to get in on the fun. Still believing that a grid system for curves eliminates redrafting and offers control and easy templates—all special advantages to the quilter—I realized the need for an additional kind of curved patch.

Phase Three as a Starting Point

Feel free to pick up the story here. Even if you have not yet tried curved patchwork, you can start with *Cutting Up With Curves.* This book contains designs, ideas and tips that you can try without committing yourself to a complex, expensive bed quilt. The design diagrams will show you which ones use only the basic system and which include the new features discussed below. You may want to experiment with the elongated and constructed curves right from the beginning. To encourage you to do so, let me say that several of the photographed items are the quilters' first projects with the Curved Two-Patch System.

Elongated Curves in a Rectangle

For realistic shapes of animals, birds, plant life and objects in our world, elongated curved patches must be used as well as the basic ones of the system (Fig. 1). While the original curves form a square, their cousins form a rectangle. In *Curves Unlimited* I broached the subject of the Curved Two-Patch arc in a rectangle, but its only in this book that patterns employ the new curves. Because it's necessary to distinguish them from the system's original and still basic curves, I call the added pair of patches the new or elongated curves.

It's obvious that an elongated curve is important for a giraffe's neck, but look at the two floral motifs in Fig. 2 to see the subtle difference between the use of the original curves and the new ones. The flower petals and leaves in Fig. 2a are fatter than those of Fig. 2b. Notice in Fig. 2c that the original curves are so short that one side of the leaf must have a straight edge. When the new curves are used (Fig. 2d), the entire edge has a subtle bend.

I don't have a magic method to convince you that the elongated curves are as easy to sew as the basic ones, but consider the common sense of it. If you've tried the original system's shallow curves, you probably found them easier to sew than the deeper, quarter-circle patches of the *Drunkard's Path.* The arc of the new, elongated pair is not as deep as the original! So you should find the new curves even easier to sew than the original ones.

In Section 5 there are various sizes of templates to trace when you need the elongated pair of curves. I've tried to draw all the sizes required for the design motifs of this book.

To draw an elongated pair of curves in a size not illustrated among the templates, I suggest you forget using a compass. The method is a rather cumbersome one for which you may have little patience. (See *Curves Unlimited* for instructions if you want to use a compass.) It's easier to draw templates with a flexible curve, which can be purchased in an art supply shop. It's a flattened plastic tube with a lead bar encased. The tube bends to form any type of curve. The flat bottom and interior weight will hold the chosen shape while you draw the curve. The principal concern in drawing templates for the elongated pair is the concave curve with one end particularly pointed. And the longer the rectangle, the skinnier the point will be on the long side

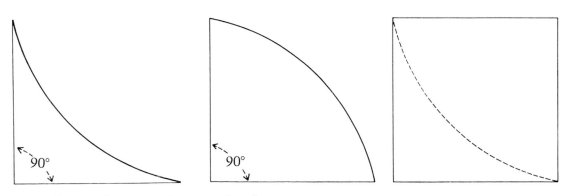

A and **B.**   The original curves that form a square.

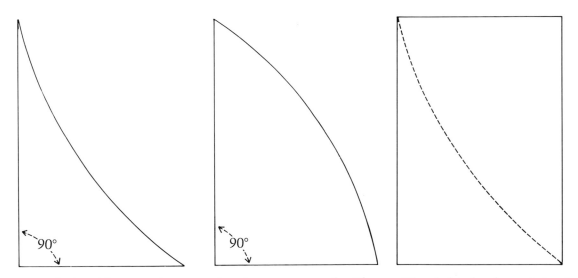

C and **D.**   Elongated curves that form a rectangle. The motifs of this book contain six different sizes of the new curves.

Fig. 1.   The Curved Two-Patch System adds an elongated set of curves. (Seam allowances are not included.)

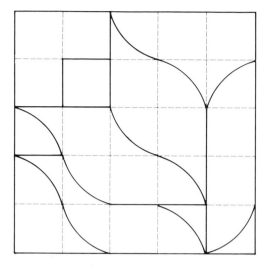

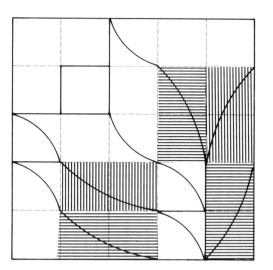

a. *Original curves form squares.*

b. *Variation with five sets of new curves forming rectangles.*

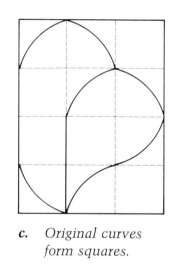

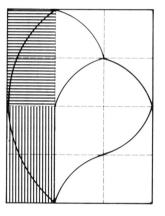

c. *Original curves form squares.*

d. *Variation with two sets of new curves forming rectangles.*

Fig. 2. *Renditions of floral designs that illustrate the slimming effect of the elongated curves that form rectangles (shaded modules).*

of the template. So let's start with that point (Fig. 3F). Draw the long side of the required rectangle vertically on template material. If you're right-handed, lay the flexible curve on the rectangle so that it intersects with the opposite corners F and H. By starting the arc at the top of what will be the concave template, you can see how

deep or shallow to make the pointed end. Tentatively start to draw the arc downwards. You may have to adjust the flexible curve. When you're satisfied that the arc you've started will give you a sewable point for a concave patch, finish drawing the curve down through corner H. (If you're left-handed, you'll have a better view of the

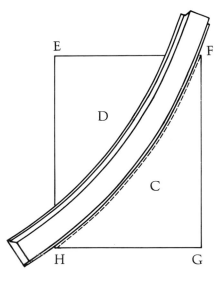

E   F

D

C

H   G

Fig. 3. *With a flexible curve, mark a gentle arc diagonally across any size of rectangle to obtain templates for elongated concave and convex curves, C and D.*

skinny point by placing the flexible curve through corners E and G.)

It's also possible to draw this new arc with a large diameter plate. But let's say you need curves from a 4″ x 8″ rectangle. You'll be hunting for something much larger to draw the arc. Here's a new use for a circular quilting hoop! It may seem strange to draw a short arc with such a huge object, but the portion of the circle that will bisect a rectangle into concave and convex curves is only a very small segment of the circumference, much less than a quarter circle. You won't be able to adjust the arc as much as you can with the flexible curve discussed above, but the hoop will let you draw an acceptable arc for any rectangle where the ratio of the sides is 2 to 1. This is the most common type of rectangle in the patterns of Section 2.

By now you can see that the depth of the arc in a rectangle is quite variable, unlike the original arc of a square which is drafted to maintain the same degree of roundness.

Depending upon your design, you may want to test the roundness of the elongated arc by cutting some paper patches as samples. Because the arc is elongated in a rectangle, it will always be fairly shallow. But the drawing method you use may cause it to flatten out almost to a straight line. Draw an obvious curve! Don't leave others to guess the shape of your patchwork and perhaps to conclude, "Poor thing can't sew a straight line!"

Constructed Curves

These are curves that have internal patches. Any curved patch, whether it's a convex or concave of either the basic or elongated pair, can be cut from other patchwork. You can cut curves from strip piecing, Seminole patchwork, crazy piecing, log cabin blocks, etc. Such double-piecing is mainly a device to add extra interest to patchwork. If you look at the color photo of *Allegro*, you'll see two examples of this idea. I pieced several nine-patch blocks and cut concave and convex patches from them. Then I pieced the curves together. In other words, the construction was done in two steps. I used the same technique for the horizontal and vertical bars in the same quilt. For this area, I started with strip-pieced yardage and then cut and sewed curves. Double pieced, double pleasure. It was exciting to use straight-edged patches as a foil for the curves. You may find other patchwork appropriate to cut into curves and to visually enrich your work.

I have a special reason for advocating the idea of constructed curves. New quilters and those trying the curved system for the first time often elect to use the larger curved templates for their first project. Being apprehensive, the gears of the mind mesh to turn out the advice: Use the largest templates. It'll be easier. There are times, however, when large, solid fabric patches cover too much area of the project. When this happens with a pattern piece for a garment, it helps to add piping on a collar, decorative buttons, pockets or some kind of embellishment. A wall hanging pieced with large poster patches, as I call them, can be boring. Such patches make up quickly and cover lots of square inches of a blank wall, but without the intrigue of details, maybe you could just give the wall a fresh coat of paint. I recommend you have a motive other than speed and ease for choosing large, curved templates. The urge to try double piecing is a good reason.

rims will not vary. Unless needed for assembly, the constructed curve is an option that's new to the system. Several of the diagramed motifs and short subjects in Section 2 feature these special curves. You might consider their use retroactively too. They work with some of the floral and abstract designs in my previous books. Refer to Fig. 4 to see suggestions.

Jigsaw Assembly

When I first wrote about the assembly method for curved designs, I advised beginners to sew concave and convex patches

a. **Bluet** from **The Curved Two-Patch System.** *Some curves cut from log cabin blocks and crazy piecing.*

b. **Crown and Orb** from **Curves Unlimited.** *Some curves cut from strip piecing.*

Fig. 4. *Constructed curves can add interest to selected floral and abstract designs.*

Occasionally a design demands a constructed curve for assembly purposes. In *Sent With Love* (see the working diagram in Section 2), several of the curves contain an extra patch so that the width of the hearts'

into square units, and then to assemble the units vertically and horizontally. More patches are cut this way, but row assembly eliminates setting in patches. Many self-confident quilters have paid little heed and cut various curved combinations. I've heard more than one say of their project with curves, "I put it together just like a jigsaw puzzle." Good! I'm glad that quilters adjust the assembly method to fit their style. In workshops I like to point out that assembly is flexible. But I've learned to tell myself: Joyce, forget all that flexible stuff for now. Show them how to start. It's more comfortable to start with a basic rule and then, in practice, learn when to break it and revise the construction for labor-saving combinations.

sizes of curves in squares and rectangles. Diversity of shapes within a design suggests assembly by modules. Let's use the *Quilt Bee* as an example (Fig. 5). The motif doesn't have any special geometric shapes, but it contains both the original and elongated curves. Although the wings and body are cut up, the outlined modules include practical combinations of patches. The assembly may be a jigsaw of squares and rectangles, but it's logical. It still adheres to the original guideline: First, sew the curves into squares and, as in the bee, into rectangles.

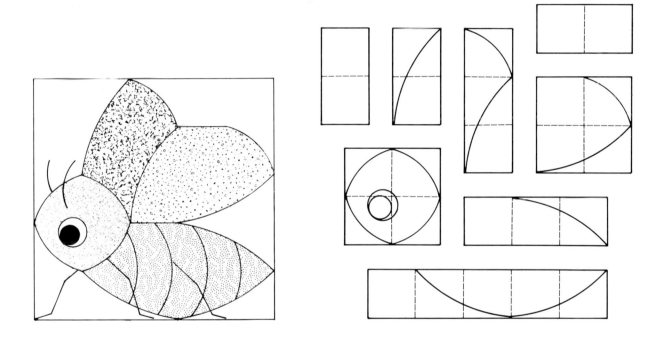

Fig. 5. *Jigsaw assembly of the **Quilt Bee** motif offers the opportunity to combine patches.*

Assembly by rows is still possible for the simpler motifs of this book; however, this construction plan became less practical when I expanded the system to include other geometric shapes in *Curves Unlimited*. Now the rule must give way for the more complex designs that contain not only other geometric shapes but also multiple

As you will find with the other motifs, the illustrated method of assembly isn't the only way, or a case of right or wrong, but what modules you feel are sensible for sewing. On the other hand, jigsaw assembly does require that you mentally "walk through" the plan first. Read about "Assembly Planning" in the next section.

In Summary

The Curved Two-Patch System: Debut

1. Shallow concave and convex curves are sewn into square units.

2. Units of curves with other squares and rectangles develop designs.

3. Assembly is by rows or columns.

4. With templates supplied, no redrafting is necessary.

5. Blocks, borders and quilts are floral patterns.

Curves Unlimited: Refinements

1. The arc for curved patches is newly determined by the diagonal of the square.

2. Designs include multiple scales of curves.

3. When straight-edged patches are included in designs, assembly is by modules.

4. New templates supplied.

5. Blocks, borders and quilts are abstract patterns.

Cutting Up With Curves: Phase Three

1. Elongated curves (forming rectangles) are added to the system.

2. Elongated and original curves are combined in designs.

3. Several designs include constructed curves (curves cut from other patchwork).

4. Jigsaw assembly.

5. Templates supplied for elongated and original curves.

6. Motifs and short subjects are mostly pictorial.

Charted Curves

SECTION TWO

*A Curved Two-Patch block
made by Janet Gillespie*

" 'The time has come,' the Walrus said,
'To talk of many things:
Of shoes—and ships—and sealing-wax—
Of cabbages—and kings—
And why the sea is boiling hot—
And whether pigs have wings?' "

THROUGH THE LOOKING-GLASS
Lewis Carroll

Shoes and cabbages don't interest me much, and I've never had reason to talk of kings. But I did once design a block called *Sealing Wax* (in *Curves Unlimited*). And in this section you'll find some ships. You can make seas about them boil with curves, if you like. Among the motifs of animals, fish, fowl and plant life, there's even a pig—not with wings, but winsome enough.

This collection of charted curves started purely as a pastime. With no serious intentions, I began to sketch curved forms that I observed or saw illustrated, whether they were man-made objects or forms from aquatic life, the farm, zoo or forest. Whatever piqued my curiosity, such as the *Sweet-smelling Skunk.* You've probably seen the cartoon of a skunk featured on a poster that says, "A friend is someone who knows all about you and likes you anyway." I saw it on the wall at the printer's everytime I visited the shop. The artist had depicted a creature so oblivious to his own anti- social behavior that I smiled each time I saw the poster. I must have commented about it often, because one day the bookkeeper took it down and, mercifully, saying no more than "Here!" she handed it to me. And so I doodled on graph paper until a sewable likeness of the unflappable fellow emerged. I found I could indulge in this grid game almost anywhere. It doesn't even require preplanning like patchwork does. If I have a layover in an airport or I'm con-

fined to any waiting area, I often amuse myself by finding some object to convert to curves-on-a-grid. The waiting period usually passes before I find a satisfactory rendition, but the idea is recorded for a later day when it's more fun to doodle than do chores and when I'm still undecided about what fabric to cut into next.

It was so much fun developing realistic subjects that I decided to make a potpourri of designs available as motifs and short subjects for quilters who want something light-hearted and brief for their next project. For "another" project, I should say, to accurately reflect today's quilters who may already have a prodigious number of works-in-progress. Some of the quilters' small works are true miniatures. Others, while larger than a breadbox, are certainly smaller than a bed quilt. Sometimes the reason for beginning yet another project is to try a new technique. Maybe it's a desire to have an alternate for a large, time-consuming quilt. For the after-work-hours quilter, it's the limited craft time in a life that's already too full. And some quilters take on one project after another because they just can't help it!

The pictorial motifs of this section can be what you make of them. You'll see two quilt guild logos converted into curved patchwork for use as banners. Your group might adopt the *Quilt Bee.* An animal motif with a simple border of fabric strips is suitable to decorate not only a child's room but also a pediatrician's waiting room. A vase of flowers in the form of a quilted hanging will enliven bland walls for someone in a nursing home. Consider making a banner with a pig motif to alert visitors before entering a teenager's room. Make a sweat shirt with the football design for the spouse who's an addict of the game. For yourself, create a studio sign with your initials. There are also a few designs appropriate for expanding into a bed quilt, such as *Pine Tree, Eight Wines* and *Fresh Blooms in a Basket.*

Several of the short subjects are originals by other quilt designers who have kindly offered projects that you might try. Each of the designers' works illustrated here depicts another's style and adds some diversity to the selection. To see more imaginative originals by still other designers, refer to the photographed projects. You'll also find a number of ideas illustrated in Section 4.

Images and Blueprints

Most of the charted curves in this section are illustrated twice. The first drawing of each subject is the image or picture of the patchwork. The second is the working diagram, usually printed to the right of the image. As spacing requires, the second diagram is occasionally below and at times on the facing page. Like a blueprint, it contains construction information. Solid assembly lines suggesting modules for piecing are superimposed on the design. Whenever an area lacks a solid line, a grid of dashes shows you how the design is broken into units. Many of the working diagrams also have shaded areas (Fig. 6) which identify constructed and elongated curves. Below the working diagrams is the number of units within the design and code letters to tell you what additional aspects of the Curved Two-Patch System have been added. (The alphabet, numerals and *Tette gouche Autumn* have obvious assemblies and do not require working diagrams.)

 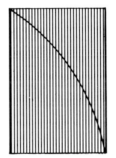

a. *Wavy lines shade constructed curves.*   ***b.*** *Straight lines shade elongated curves.*

Fig. 6. *The working diagrams include two types of shading to distinguish constructed and elongated curves.*

Inches or Centimeters for Units

A unit, the basic module of a design, equals one square of the grid regardless of the apparent size of that grid. (Some designs have been enlarged for more visual significance.) The system's basic curves fit within one unit. Whenever a curve covers more than one unit, it is either a multiple scale of the original pair of curves or this book's additional set of elongated curves that fit into a rectangle (shaded, as mentioned above).

I want to emphasize that the number of units per design does not refer to specific measurements. It identifies the smallest scale of curves with which you'll work. Decide what size of curved patch will be comfortable to sew. Choose inches or centimeters. Then multiply the number of units in the design by your chosen patch size. This determines the dimensions of the finished patchwork. Let's use one of the curved numeral designs as an example. Each is 3 x 4 units. You've decided to work with 2" (5cm) curves. Therefore, each pieced numeral will finish to 6" x 8" (15cm x 20cm). If you've chosen to construct one of the short subjects, I've supplied either the dimensions used by the quilter or suggested a specific size for the project.

Letter Code

To help you analyze the patchwork designs, I've added a letter code below the working diagrams whenever new features have been included with the basic concave and convex curves. If there are no code letters present, the design can be constructed with the three basic patches: a concave, a convex and their matching square. (Also see code D below.)

Code C. Constructed Curve. The term refers to either a concave or convex patch that is a composite of pieces. When such a curved patch is cut from strip piecing, the code letter appears only as a suggestion and double piecing is optional. However, in a few designs, one of the curves must be constructed. See *Mouse in a T-shirt* for an example. Constructed curves are shaded with wavy lines. (See Fig. 6.)

Code D. Detail to Embroider or Applique. The floral designs of *The Curved Two-Patch System* had a bit of embroidery to enhance them. The abstract designs in *Curves Unlimited* didn't need any. Now returning to pictorial images, I've listed this code letter to indicate the need of an eye, legs, whiskers, or even a ship's mast. So even simple-to-piece designs may call for this kind of detailing.

Code E. Elongated Curves (*Multiple Sizes). The straight- lined shading of elongated curves makes their presence obvious in a design. And, indeed, the code letter for the simpler designs is only a reminder. When there are several pairs of elongated curves in a pattern, the code letter by itself assures you that all use the same size of templates. When the code letter is followed by an asterisk, the design has varying sizes of the elongated curves. Count the units covered by each pair of curves to discover how many sizes of templates you need. Also be aware that in a few patterns one of the curves is not only elongated but also constructed and, therefore, shaded with wavy lines. But the matching curve is shaded with straight lines to say that the two elongated curves form a rectangle. This is true of *Patchwork Balloon, Sanderlings, A Bell Pull* and *Fresh Blooms in a Basket*.

Code M. Multiple Sizes of the Basic Curves. This code letter indicates that you will need at least two sizes of templates for the basic curves. Large scale curves cover more than one unit of the grid. Typically they're double scale and cover 2 x 2 units. A few are 3 x 3 units. The code letter has some overlaps: In *Kiosk*, the large arc for the tent's top covers 4 x 4 units, but I also suggest making it of constructed curves. There is a double-scaled curve in *Sent With Love* that is constructed too. When there are two reasons for marking a particular curve, the design carries both code letters.

In these cases the code at the bottom includes both C and M.

Code T. Template to Draft. Don't let this code letter deter you from choosing a design. The letter refers to a few conventional shapes, such as narrow strips or triangles cut from squares. The parallelograms for *Stacked Deck* and the shape of the cabin for *Seaworthy* are the most elaborate templates expected. The code letter, however, does not signify optional combination templates. Use the system's templates to form multiple shapes. For more about common combinations, refer to Section 3 and the group of templates at the end of the book.

Assembly Planning

As mentioned earlier, the simpler motifs and short subjects that can be constructed in rows or columns do not have special assembly diagrams. All other designs have solid lines super- imposed on working diagrams to indicate plausible divisions for sewing. In each case I tried to mark a logical assembly with modules that permit some practical combinations of curves. Take some time to study the assembly plan to see whether or not you want to make changes.

If you are unaccustomed to reading such a printed plan, think of it as finished patchwork that you're going to take apart. You must work backwards, from the last seam to the first. Look for an edge strip of patches, which would be the last portion to join. If there is one, cover it with a sheet of paper to avoid distraction. Next look for a long line that goes through the remainder or at least a major portion of the design. (I established at least one major division, even if it cuts through a favored combination of

curves. Its purpose is to avoid right-angled seams or set-in corners.) Let your eyes and free hand outline the perimeter of this large section, a square or rectangle. Again cover other portions of the design so your attention is concentrated. Within this major division, identify medium-size squares and rectangles of patches that fit together with straight seams. Examine the curves and other shapes within each medium-size module to determine what combinations you want to cut for patches. You're in the heart of the design where you're deciding the first seams. Also examine the remaining design portions in this same manner. You're ready now to retrace your steps and number the sewing order as you return from the interior to the outside edge of the design and the last strip of patches. After practicing once or twice, you'll be surprised how quickly your eye becomes trained at this deciphering game.

During the examination of the illustrated assembly, you may have decided on a quite different plan of attack. Within the modules, you may want to combine more patches for fewer seams or to cut more single curves to avoid having to make odd-shaped templates. Here's a guideline to keep in mind if you're planning a new assembly: The more curves combined in one patch, the more the assembly becomes like a jigsaw rather than a row or column construction. It's advisable to block out your final decision on tracing paper laid over the working diagram. Leave some space between the tracings of each section. Then number the segments for a sewing order. This visual map may spotlight some awkwardness of construction, which can be easily solved with a good eraser. If you've decided to follow the printed assembly, allow yourself to number the sewing order directly in your own book. A book owner should enjoy this privilege.

Motifs: Curves in Our World

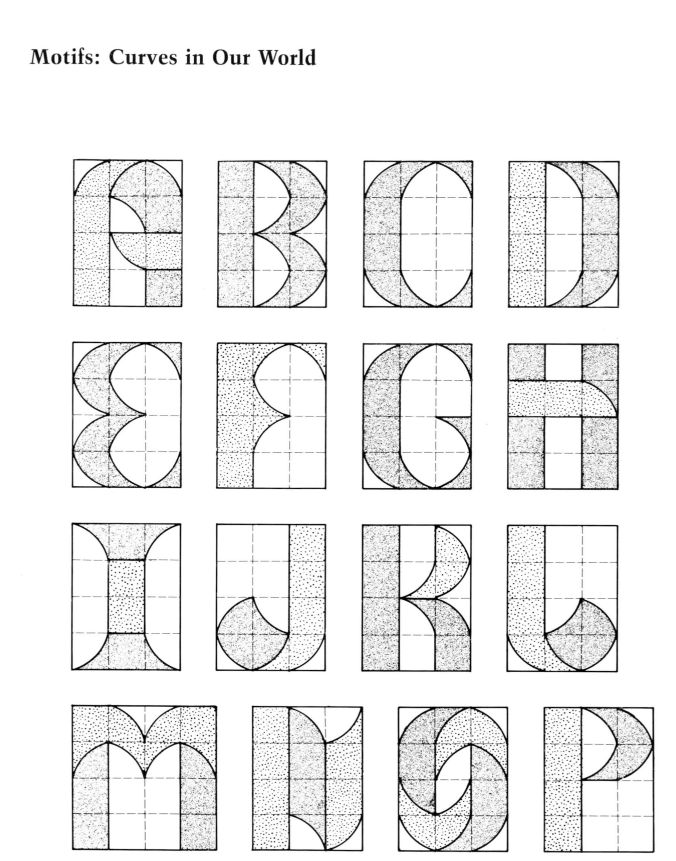

*All letters and numerals are 3 × 4 units, except "**M**" and "**W**" which are 4 × 4 units. Assemble units in rows or columns.*

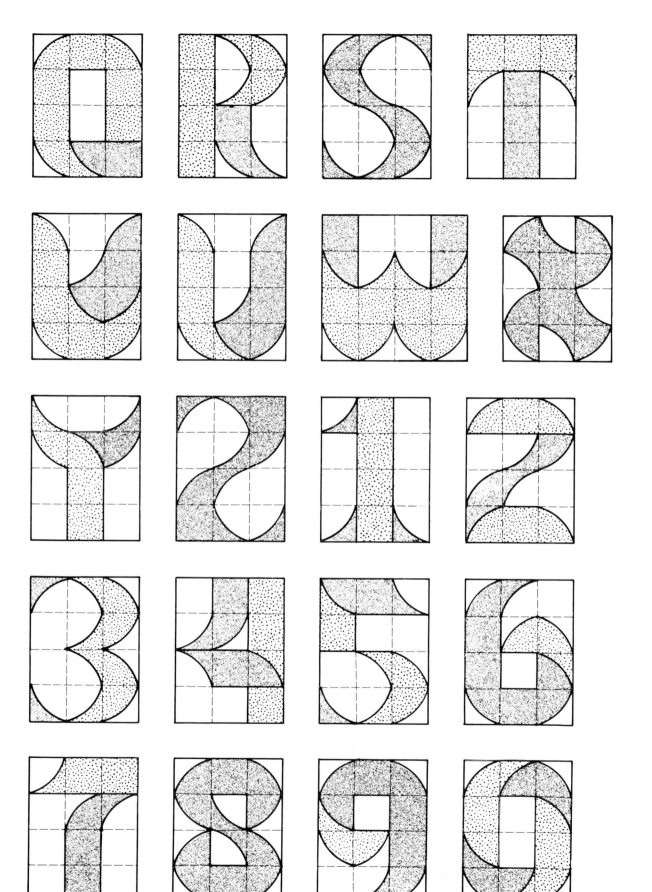

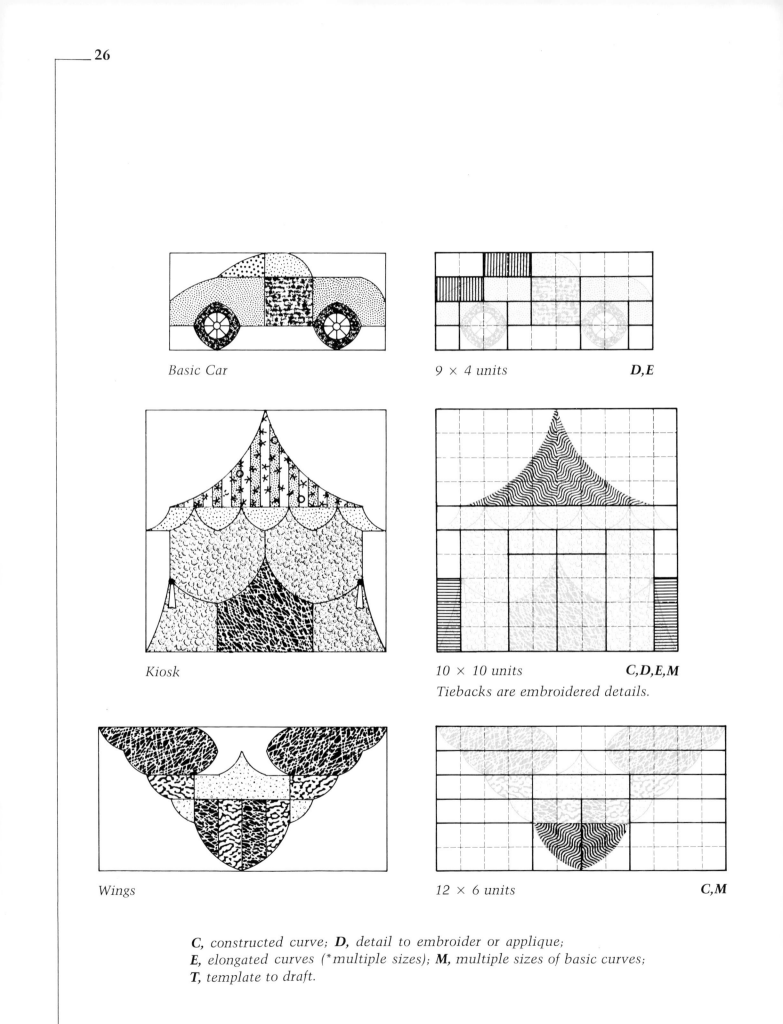

Basic Car

9 × 4 units   **D,E**

Kiosk

10 × 10 units   **C,D,E,M**

Tiebacks are embroidered details.

Wings

12 × 6 units   **C,M**

C, *constructed curve;* **D,** *detail to embroider or applique;*
E, *elongated curves (*multiple sizes);* **M,** *multiple sizes of basic curves;*
T, *template to draft.*

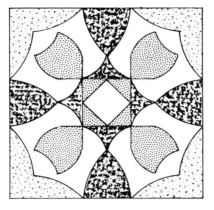

Eight Wines

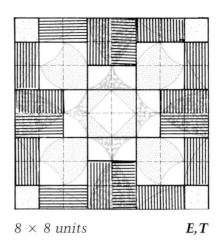

8 × 8 units   ***E, T***

Fleur-de-lis

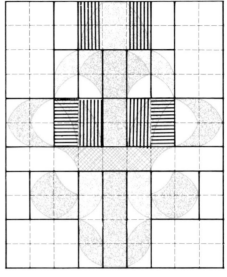

9 × 11 units   ***E***

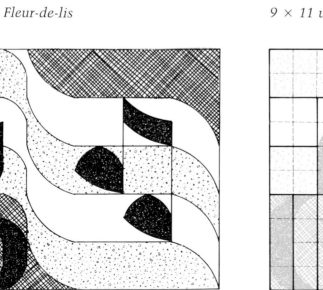

Music Lover's Sign

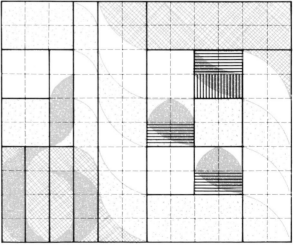

12 × 10 units   ***D, E, M***

Embroidery is along seam lines.

C, *constructed curve;* ***D,*** *detail for embroidery or applique;*
E, *elongated curves (*multiple sizes);* ***M,*** *multiple sizes of basic curves;*
T, *template to draft.*

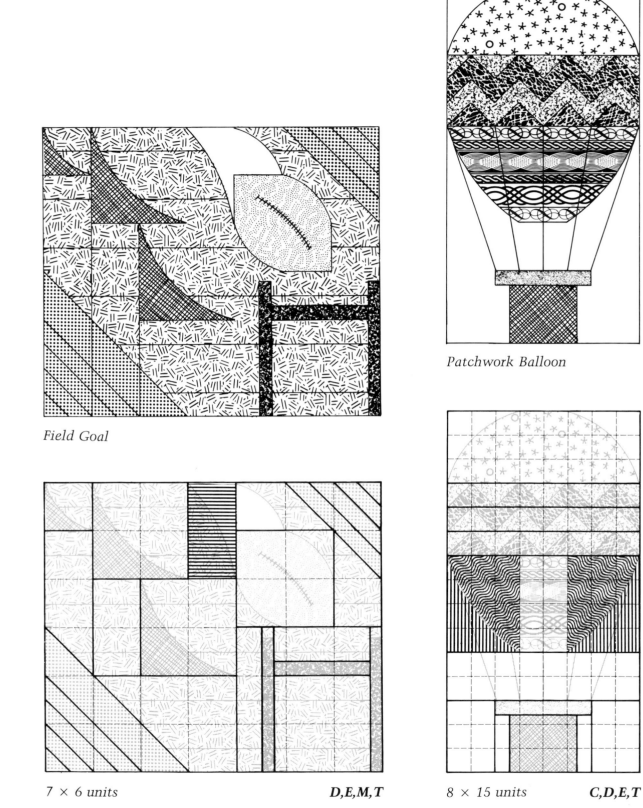

Field Goal

Patchwork Balloon

7 × 6 units **D,E,M,T**

8 × 15 units **C,D,E,T**

Embroidered field markings horizontally bisect the units.

C, constructed curve; D, detail for embroidery or applique;
E, elongated curves (*multiple sizes); M, multiple sizes of basic curves;
T, template to draft.

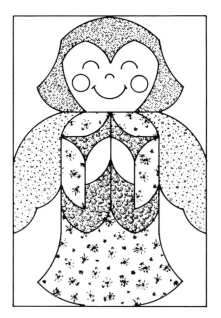

Angel Doll

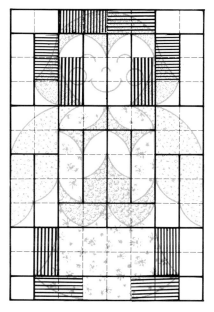

8 × 12 units　　　　**D,E,M**

Sunbonnet Sue, Herself

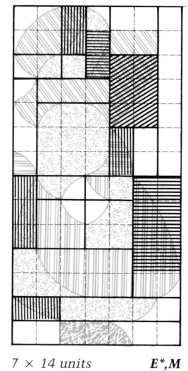

7 × 14 units　　　　**E*,M**

C, *constructed curve;* **D,** *detail for embroidery or applique;*
E, *elongated curves (*multiple sizes);* **M,** *multiple sizes of basic curves;*
T, *template to draft.*

Fresh Blooms in a Basket

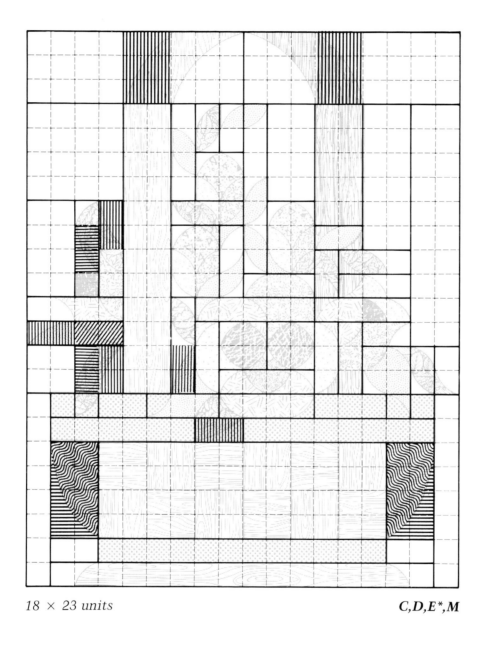

18 × 23 units   **C,D,E*,M**

C, *constructed curves;* **D,** *detail for embroidery or applique;*
E, *elongated curves (*multiple sizes);* **M,** *multiple sizes of basic curves;*
T, *template to draft.*

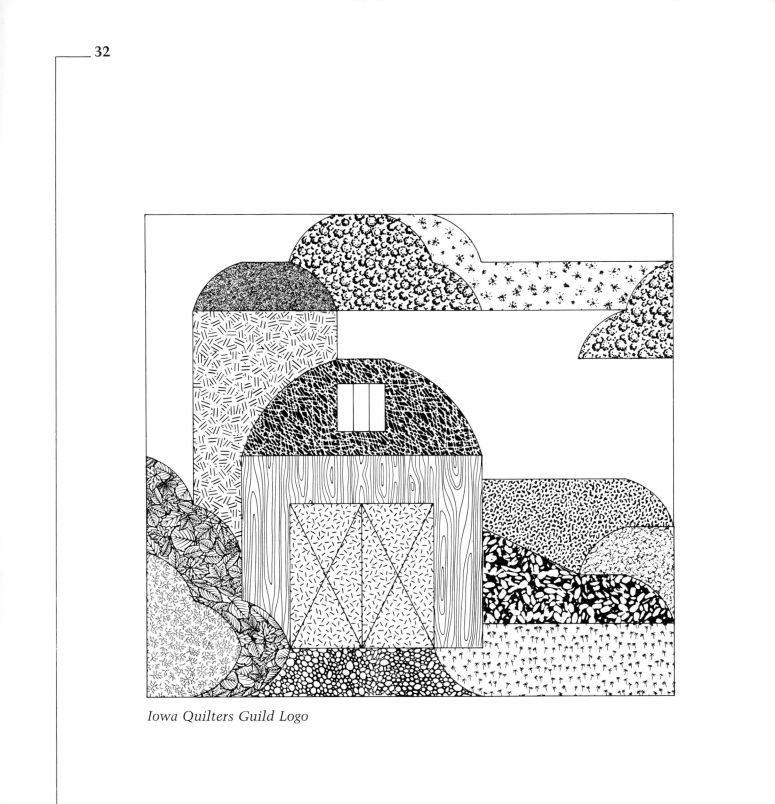

Iowa Quilters Guild Logo

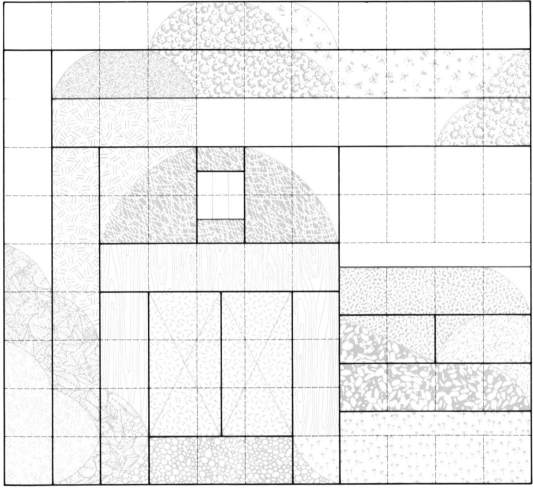

11 × 10 units   **D,M,T**

Above and below the hills, a half-unit wide strip horizontally interrupts the grid.

C, constructed curve; **D,** detail for embroidery or applique;
E, elongated curves (*multiple sizes); **M,** multiple sizes of basic curves;
T, template to draft.

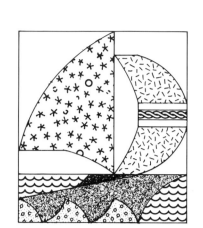

Seaworthy

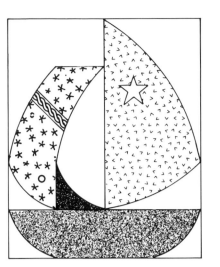

Sail Boat

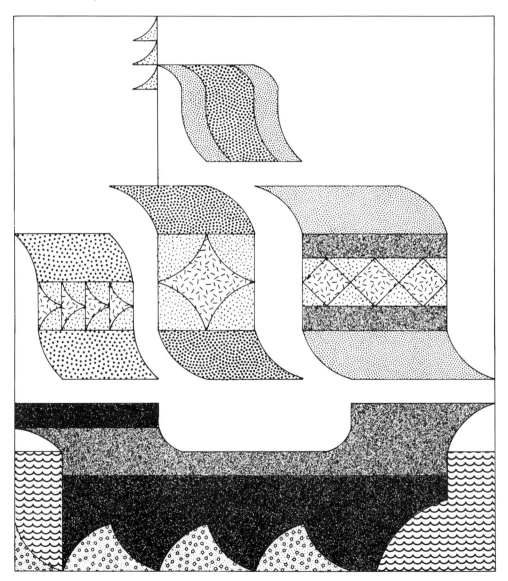

Tall Ship

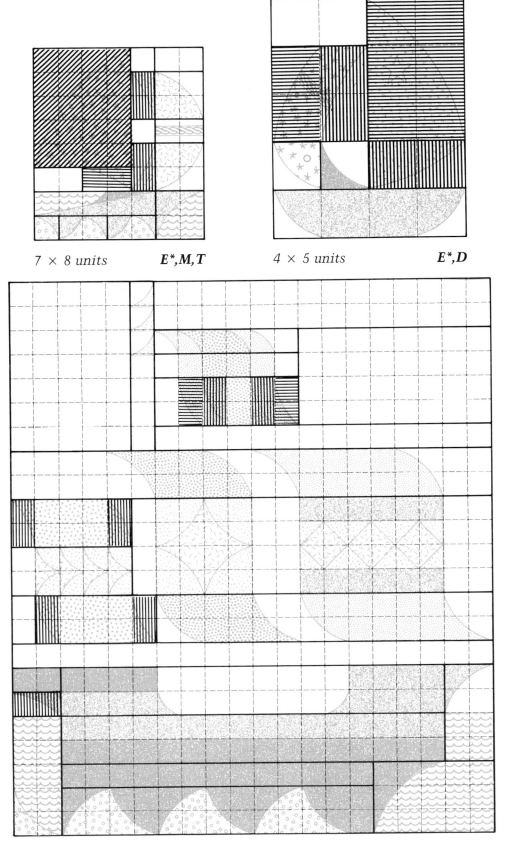

7 × 8 units   **E*,M,T**

4 × 5 units   **E*,D**

20 × 23 units   **D,E,M,T**

Embroidery is along seam lines.

C, constructed curve; **D,** detail for embroidery or applique;
E, elongated curves (*multiple sizes); **M,** multiple sizes of basic curves;
T, template to draft.

Motifs: Curves From Life About Us

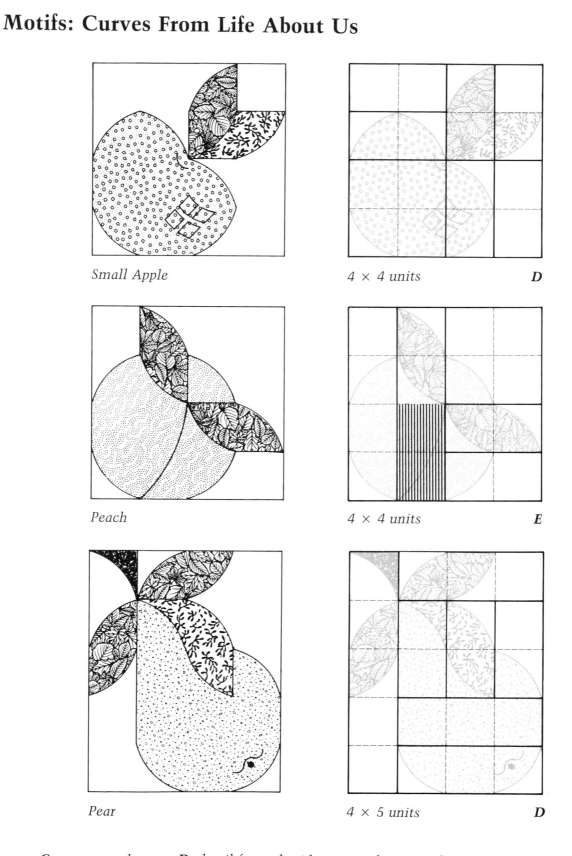

Small Apple   4 × 4 units   **D**

Peach   4 × 4 units   **E**

Pear   4 × 5 units   **D**

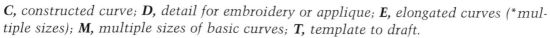

*C, constructed curve; **D**, detail for embroidery or applique; **E**, elongated curves (*multiple sizes); **M**, multiple sizes of basic curves; **T**, template to draft.*

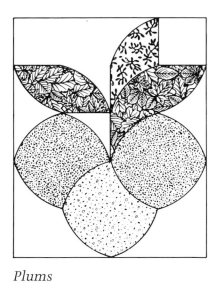

Plums

4 × 5 units

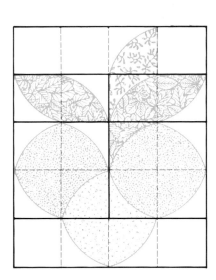

Apple with Stem

4 × 5 units   **D,M**

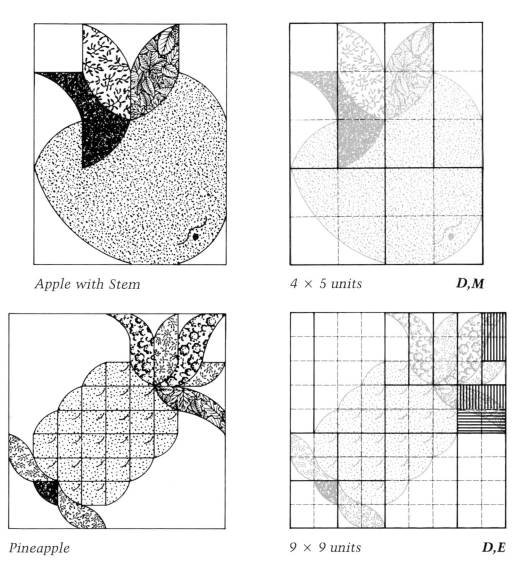

Pineapple

9 × 9 units   **D,E**

C, constructed curve; **D,** detail for embroidery or applique; **E,** elongated curves (*multiple sizes); **M,** multiple sizes of basic curves; **T,** template to draft.

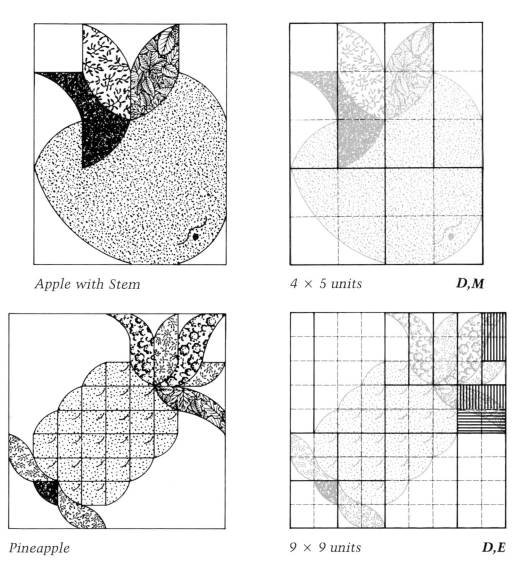

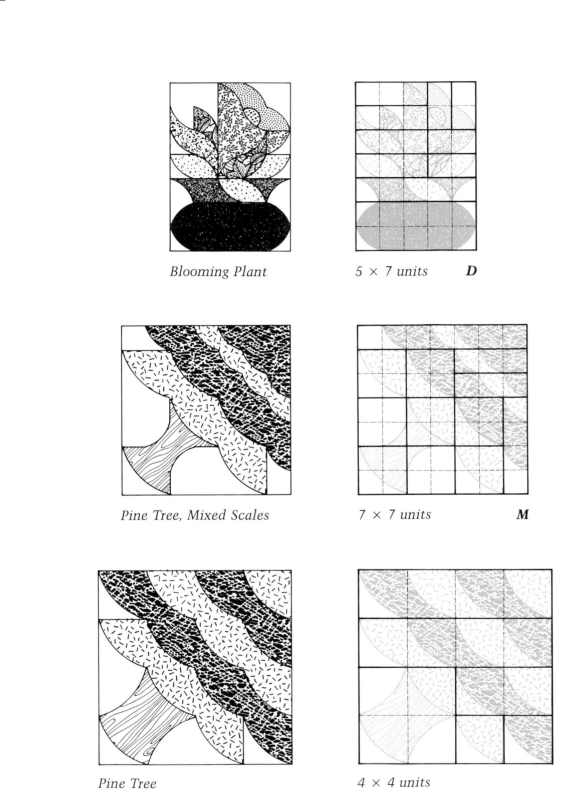

38

Blooming Plant

5 × 7 units   **D**

Pine Tree, Mixed Scales

7 × 7 units   **M**

Pine Tree

4 × 4 units

C, constructed curve; **D,** detail for embroidery or applique; **E,** elongated curves (*multiple sizes); **M,** multiple sizes of basic curves; **T,** template to draft.

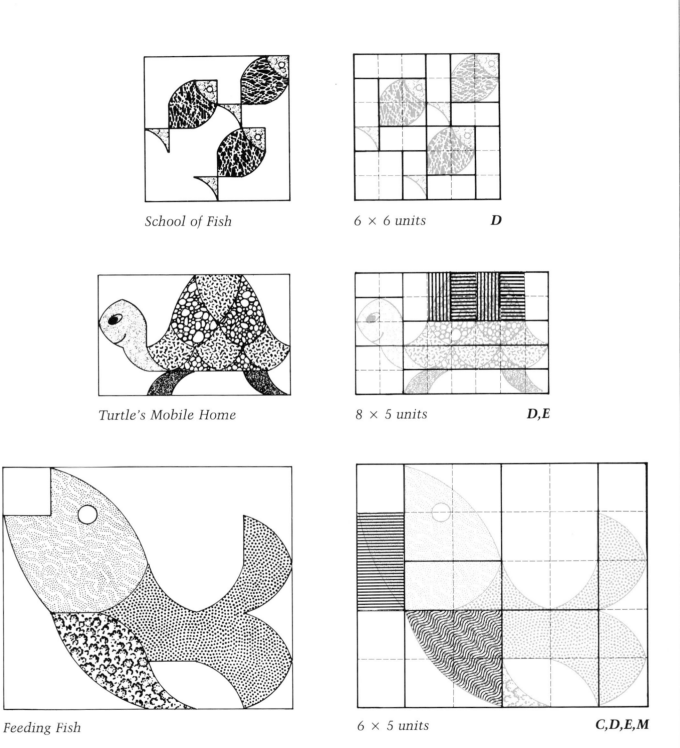

School of Fish   6 × 6 units   **D**

Turtle's Mobile Home   8 × 5 units   **D,E**

Feeding Fish   6 × 5 units   **C,D,E,M**

C, constructed curve; **D,** detail for embroidery or applique;
E, elongated curves (*multiple sizes); **M,** multiple sizes of basic curves;
T, template to draft.

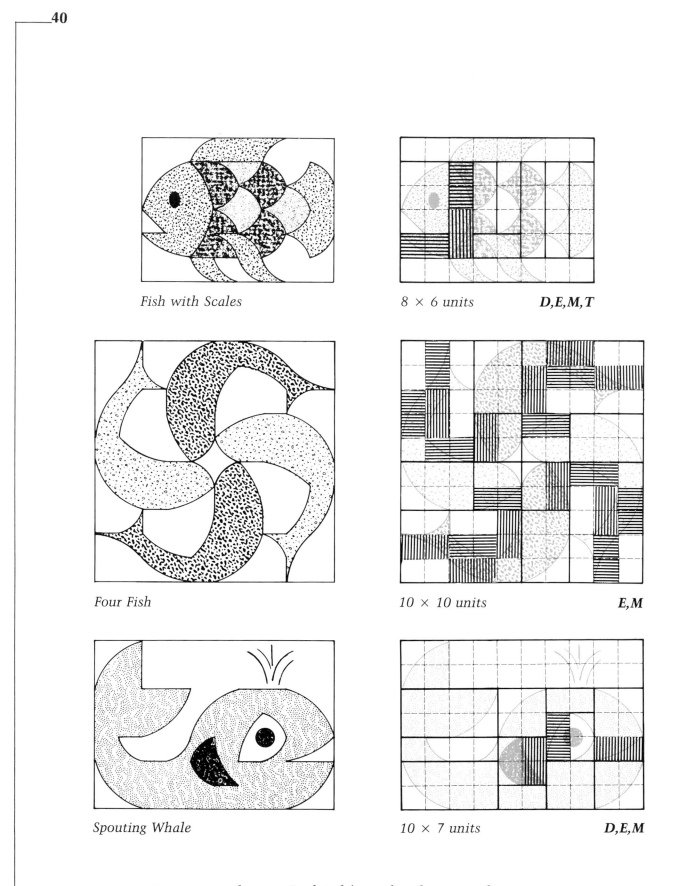

Fish with Scales   8 × 6 units   **D,E,M,T**

Four Fish   10 × 10 units   **E,M**

Spouting Whale   10 × 7 units   **D,E,M**

C, constructed curve; **D,** detail for embroidery or applique;
E, elongated curves (*multiple sizes); **M,** multiple sizes of basic curves;
T, template to draft.

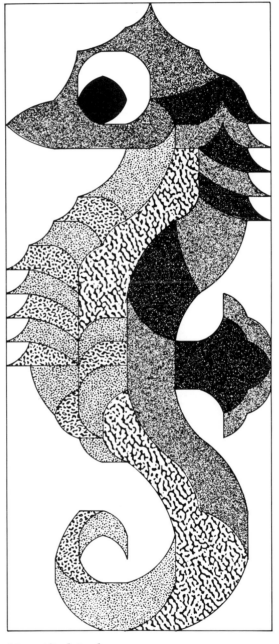

Magnified Seahorse

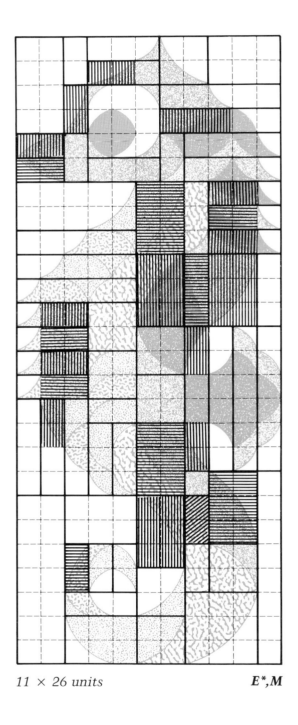

11×26 units

E**,*M

C, constructed curve; *D,* detail for embroidery or applique;
E, elongated curves (*multiple sizes); *M,* multiple sizes of basic curves;
T, template to draft.

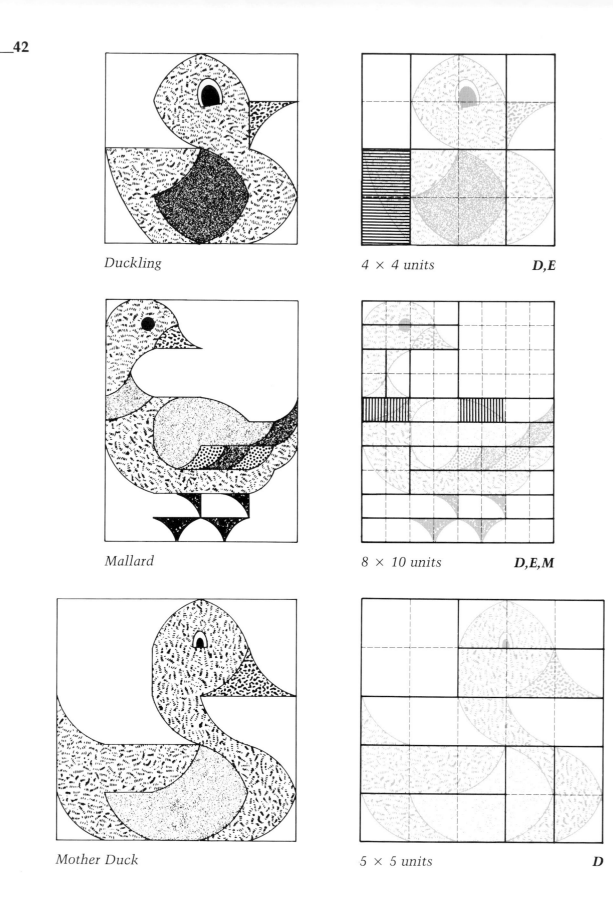

Duckling   4 × 4 units   **D,E**

Mallard   8 × 10 units   **D,E,M**

Mother Duck   5 × 5 units   **D**

C, constructed curve; **D,** detail for embroidery or applique;
E, elongated curves (*multiple sizes); **M,** multiple sizes of basic curves;
T, template to draft.

Cocksure
Based on design by Nancy Drum.

Chicklette

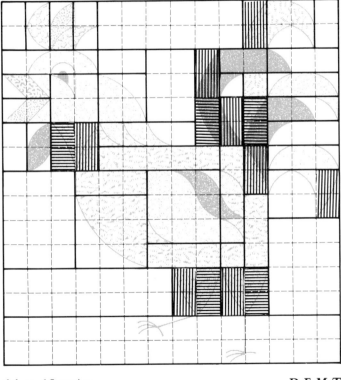

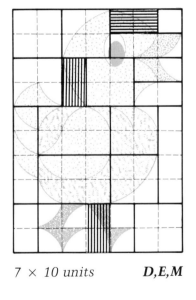

7 × 10 units   ***D,E,M***

14 × 15 units   ***D,E,M,T***
Eye to be embroidered or appliqued.

C, constructed curve; D, detail for embroidery or applique;
E, elongated curves (*multiple sizes); M, multiple sizes of basic curves;
T, template to draft.

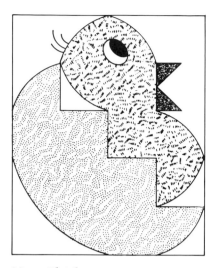

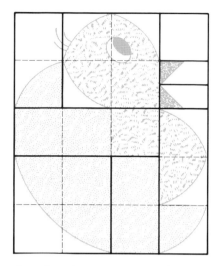

New Chick

4 × 5 units **D,M,T**

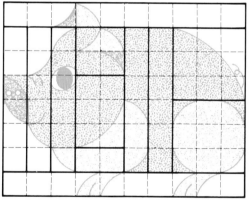

Porker

10 × 8 units **D,M**

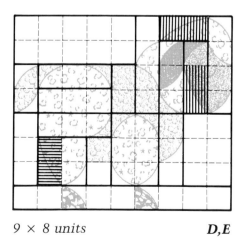

Lamb's Wool

9 × 8 units **D,E**

C, constructed curve; **D,** detail for embroidery or applique;
E, elongated curves (*multiple sizes); **M,** multiple sizes of basic curves;
T, template to draft.

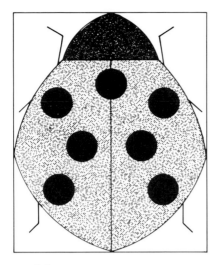

Ladybug

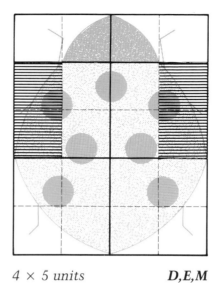

4 × 5 units   **D,E,M**

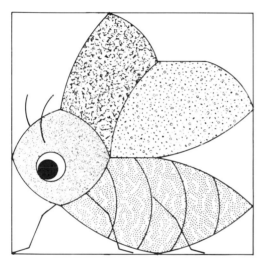

Quilt Bee

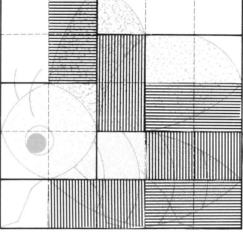

5 × 5 units   **D,E**

Resting Rabbit

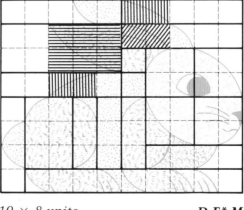

10 × 8 units   **D,E*,M**

C, *constructed curve;* **D,** *detail for embroidery or applique;*
E, *elongated curves (*multiple sizes);* **M,** *multiple sizes of basic curves;*
T, *template to draft.*

Owl, side view of body   6 × 12 units   **D,E,M**

Owl, front view   8 × 12 units   **D,E,M**
Logo for Nite Owl Quilters, Covina, CA

C, constructed curve; **D,** detail for embroidery or applique;
E, elongated curves (*multiple sizes); **M,** multiple sizes of basic curves;
T, template to draft.

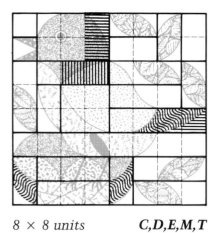

Nesting Bird

8 × 8 units **C,D,E,M,T**

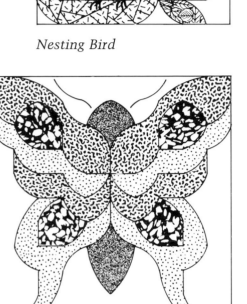

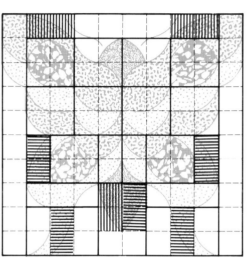

Swallowtail Butterfly

10 × 10 units **D,E**

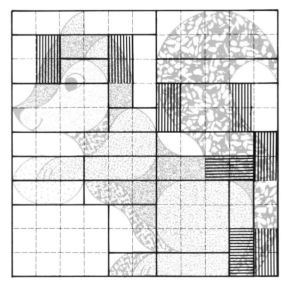

Squirrel with Snack

11 × 11 units **D,E,M**

C, constructed curve; D, detail for embroidery or applique;
E, elongated curves (*multiple sizes); M, multiple sizes of basic curves;
T, template to draft.

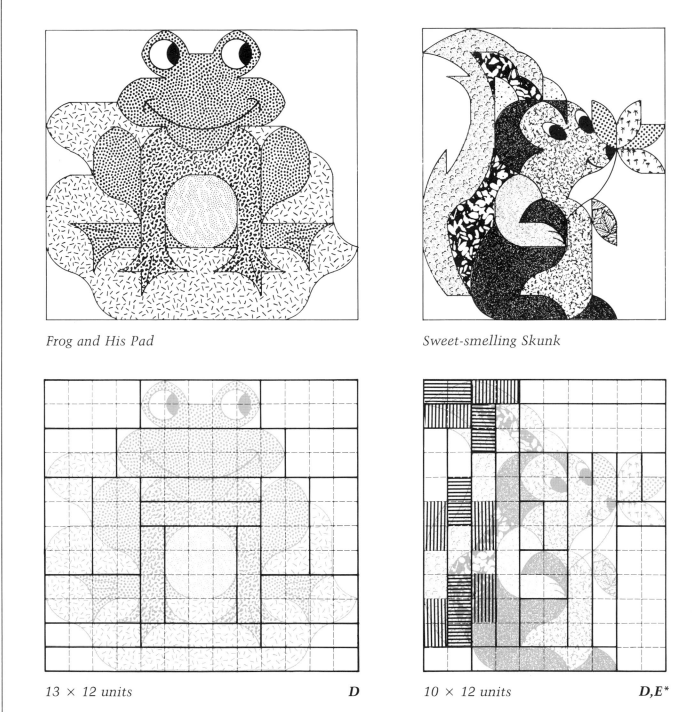

Frog and His Pad

Sweet-smelling Skunk

13 × 12 units   **D**

10 × 12 units   **D,E***

C, constructed curve; **D,** detail for embroidery or applique;
E, elongated curves (*multiple sizes); **M,** multiple sizes of basic curves;
T, template to draft.

1. Allegro, *36″ square. Designed, pieced and hand-quilted by Schlotzhauer for Silver Dollar City's Quilter's Challenge, 1987. Cotton fabrics by Springs Industries. A mix of straight-edged patches and multiple-scaled curves, some of which were cut from other patchwork.*

2. Iowa Quilters Guild Logo, *24" x 22" made by Karan Flanscha from author's design. Basic curves are 2" x 4". Hand-quilted.*

3. Cornucopia, *33" x 28½", pieced and hand-quilted by Sheri Hughes. A challenge to find fabrics for the orange, bananas and particularly the pear that would be realistic colors yet have adequate contrast. Author's design.*

4. Dress with **Blooming Plant** made by Maxine Town-send. A cream-colored fringe borders the pieced and hand-embroidered bodice. Adapted from a pattern by Coleen Walters.

5. & 6. Child's robe (above right) with **Giraffe at Lunch**. The design, pieced with patches based on 1" curves, is ap-pliqued to a velour robe. Child's sweat shirt (left) with **Spotted Pup**. Shirt front is strip-pieced. Movable plastic eyes bring the pup to life. Both garments made by Joyce Buchberger.

7. Announcing Jesse, 36" x 48", a baby gift for a new nephew. Designed, pieced and hand-quilted by Nancy Drum with the author as consultant. Curved Two-Patch basic and elongated curves in multiple sizes.

8. *The Oceans Are Alive,* *64″ × 67″, designed and made by Virginia Walton. Renditions of **Magnified Seahorse** based on 1½″ and 1¼″ curved patches. More fish in the murky depths are machine quilted.*

9. *The Game of Cat and Mouse,* *31″ x 38″. Paula Libby worked with curves of 1½″ and ¾″ in various combination patches. She modified **Curious Cat** to resemble her own "brown-mackeral tabby." Embroidered and quilted by hand.*

10. *Sanderlings, A Bell Pull,* *8″ x 39″. Designed, pieced and hand-quilted by Jean V. Johnson "to depict the little sandpiper who feeds at the water's edge." Of miniature blocks that include new features of the curved system.*

11. Dragon Lair, *60″ square, an original hand-quilted hanging by Joyce Schlotzhauer. Read how the author developed the design in Section 4, "Variations Within a Curved Motif."*

13. Cherry Blossom Girl, *18" x 46½",
an original design by Dot Stutter.
Completely machine-stitched. (Photograph supplied by the designer.)*

12. Imari Dragon, *57" x 60". Designed, pieced and hand-quilted by
Jane Blair. A mix of basic, elongated and constructed curves. Notice
how the sinuous curves of the dragons are accented by spiky borders.*

14. Valley Camp, 22" x 28". Hand-pieced and hand-quilted by Nancy Drum. Thirty-five cotton prints. Many combination patches made of both the original and elongated curves. Author's design.

15. Constantinople, 69½" x 53¾". Rita Erickson's design includes various sizes of the basic curved patches and a couple of appliqued ones. Mainly strip-pieced with hand quilting in progress.

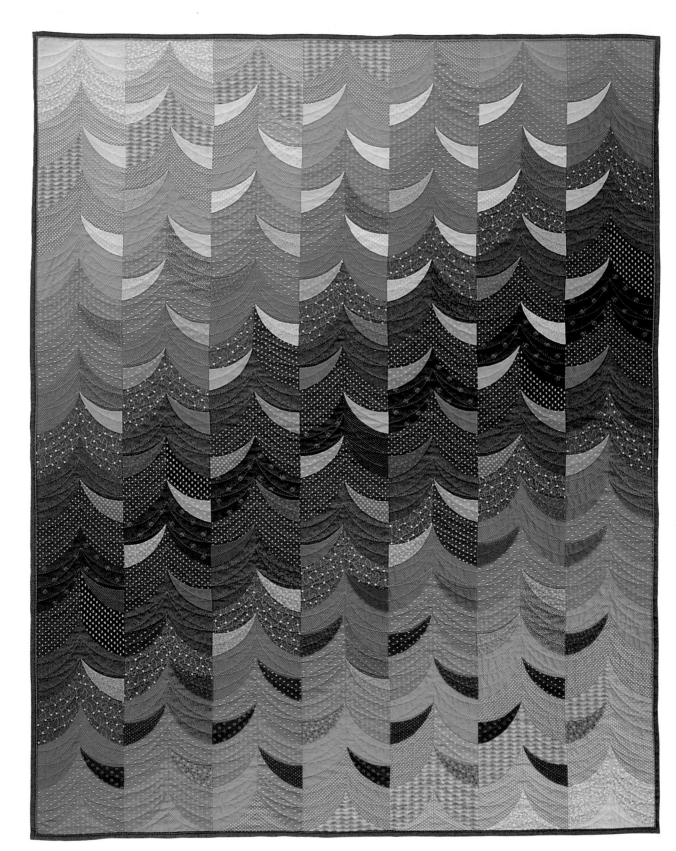

16. Tettegouche Autumn, *49" x 63", designed, pieced and hand quilted by Rosemary Root. Beginning with gradation of 12 green prints, she added some gray and bright, burning colors for the falling leaves.*

Curious Cat

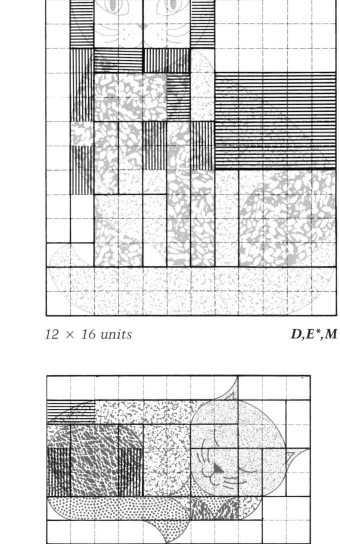

12 × 16 units   **D,E*,M**

Cat Nap

11 × 7 units   **D,E,M**

C, constructed curve; **D,** detail for embroidery or applique;
E, elongated curves (*multiple sizes); **M,** multiple sizes of basic curves;
T, template to draft.

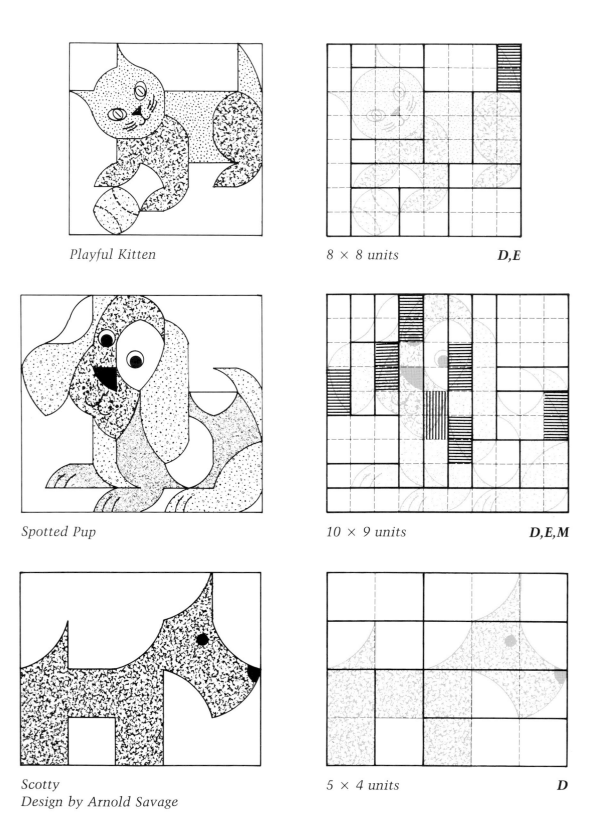

Playful Kitten

8 × 8 units   **D,E**

Spotted Pup

10 × 9 units   **D,E,M**

Scotty
Design by Arnold Savage

5 × 4 units   **D**

*C, constructed curve; **D,** detail for embroidery or applique;*
***E,** elongated curves (*multiple sizes); **M,** multiple sizes of basic curves;*
***T,** template to draft.*

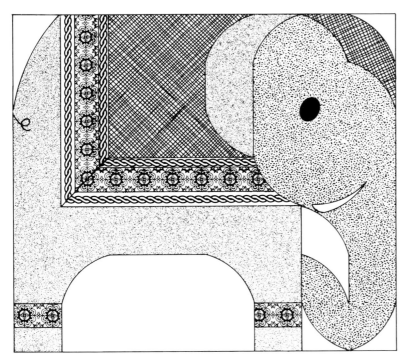

Elephant on Parade

Mouse in T-shirt

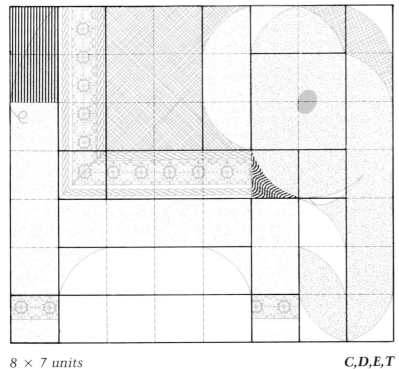

8 × 7 units   ***C,D,E,T***
Strip-pieced border of blanket is to be mitered.

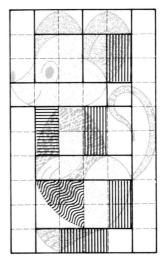

6 × 10 units   ***C,D,E,M***

       C, *constructed curve;* ***D,*** *detail for embroidery or applique;*
       E, *elongated curves (*multiple sizes);* ***M,*** *multiple sizes of basic curves;*
       T, *template to draft.*

60

Drowsy Lion

Theodore
Inspiration from design
by Suzanne Brown.

15 × 12 units   **D,E,M**

8 × 12 units   **D,E,M**

C, constructed curve; D, detail for embroidery or applique;
E, elongated curves (*multiple sizes); M, multiple sizes of basic curves;
T, template to draft.

Giraffe at Lunch

14×24 units **D,E*,M**

Two different fabrics should be chosen for giraffe's spots.

C, constructed curve; **D,** detail for embroidery or applique;
E, elongated curves (*multiple sizes); **M,** multiple sizes of basic curves;
T, template to draft.

Short Subjects

Sanderlings, A Bell Pull
Designer and quilter: Jean V. Johnson
Unit size: 1"
Dimensions: 8" x 39"
Color plate 10

Jean Johnson's miniature shore bird features a blend of the original and elongated curved patches. The latter appear not only in two sizes (½" x 1" and 1" x 2"), but a couple of the concave patches are also constructed curves. Much of the appeal of this design for a bell pull relies on details. Try to envision the bird without the extra cut in concave curves to define the delicate beak and pointed tail. Of course, in looking at the color plate, you'll discover that Jean's choice of fabric for the shore is a major de-tail that helps establish the scene.

There's no need to be concerned about the tiny patches for the legs, ½" x 1". Have you noticed that their curves don't have to match up with other curves?

Start and end the bell pull with the 6" x 7" motif shown in the larger illustration. Make one more for the design's center (not shown). Alternate the motifs with two reverse ones, 6" x 7". Then add a wave, 2" x 6", for the bottom. (The lower portion of the bell pull is illustrated to show the three modules.) Jean added a narrow light-colored frame before her final 1" border.

For another application of the little sandpiper, see Jean's interpretation for two table runners in Section 4.

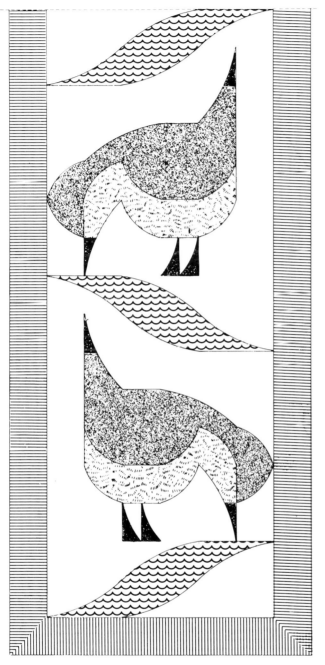

Sanderlings, A Bell Pull

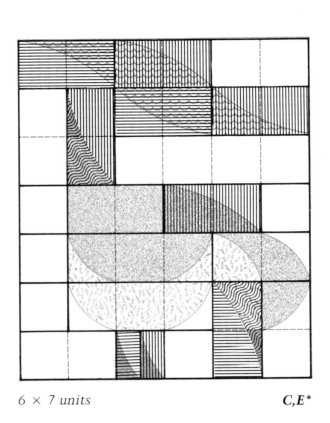

6 × 7 units   **C,E***

½" × 1"

The above miniature templates, ½" × 1" (illustrated without seam allowances and needed only for this project), are for the bird's legs. Other templates are in Section 5.

Cherry Blossom Girl

Designer and quilter: Dot Stutter
Adaptation by the author
Unit size: 1½"
Dimensions: 18" x 46½"
Color plate 13

On a trip to the west coast, I became acquainted with Dot Stutter and her almost life-size panel of an Oriental girl. It was intriguing to see how a few well-placed curves could carve out such a charming figure. Dot has kindly consented to this rendition of her pattern.

The additional templates for this piece include the elongated curves (1½" x 3") and a constructed curve for the sandals. A template for the sandals and patterns for the appliqued flowers for the hair are provided in Section 5.

You'll have fun with the fan. There are many interpretations that will focus attention to it. Decorate it with embroidery or appliques. Consider strip piecing it with wedge-shaped patches. Or use a scrap of light-weight drapery fabric with a pictorial pattern. To make a template for half of the fan (a module of the assembly diagram), draw a 4½" square and use the two sizes of the basic curved templates to trace the arcs. Then add the diagonal with a ruler.

The chin in this rendition is blunt. If that bothers you, use Dot Stutter's idea of rounding it off with the convex of the elongated curves. Whatever your decision, I feel that a seam between the face and neck is important for definition.

The keyhole border can be pieced or appliqued. With ⅜" strips, the "holes" in the corners will be ¾" squares; however, the diagram shows somewhat wider strips. As a result, the holes are smaller.

Cherry Blossom Girl

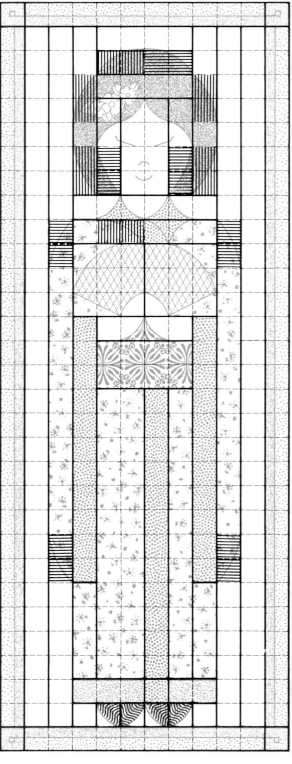

12 × 31 units   ***C,D,E,M,T***

Cornucopia

Cornucopia
Quilter: Sheri Hughes
Design by the author
Unit size: 1½"
Dimensions: 33" x 28½"
Color plate 3

Choosing a project smaller than a bed quilt does not have to limit a quilter to fewer fabrics. On the contrary. This wall hanging should satisfy the quilter who enjoys the interaction of many fabrics and much color. By my count, you'll find use for at least 18 fabrics. The cornucopia needs three, as do the leaves where several touch each other. Choose two fabrics each for the pineapple squares, the pair of bananas and the plums. (They're plums only because I say so.) I recommend that you decide on a background fabric first, because other color choices must advance while it recedes.

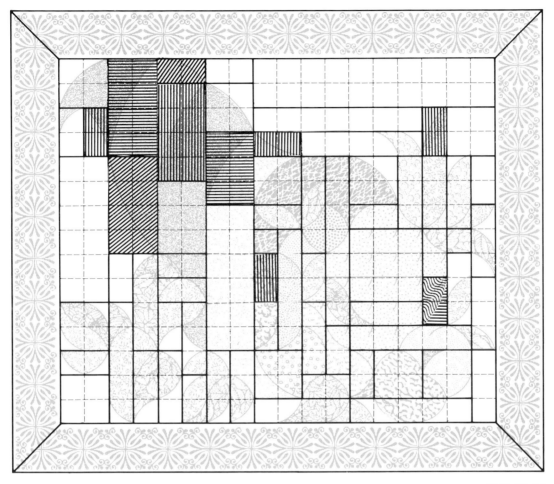

22 × 19 units   **C,D,E*,M**

The left side of the assembly is planned for vertical strips to accommodate the various scales of elongated curves in rectangles. With fruit-salad pieces cutting up the right side, you can alternate fabrics for the pineapple chunks and still use combination patches to nestle the other edibles into the picture.

Don't miss seeing the lone concave patch that belongs to the bottom of the cornucopia. It's located below the pineapple, between the pear and apple.

This design requires three sets of elongated curves: 1½″ x 3″, 3″ x 4½″ and 3″ x 6″. The border shown is two units wide.

A Dozen Plus

A Dozen Plus
Quilter: Ruth Him
Design by the author
Unit size: 2"
Dimensions: 32" x 58"
Photo on back cover

No code letters are necessary for the urn of roses. The entire design employs the basic Curved Two-Patch System. With only three templates necessary, this is one of the easiest short subjects in this section.

Sometime ago I asked Ruth Him to construct the bouquet for me. Ruth used even more reds than required, strip pieced the fluted vase and, where the border meets the

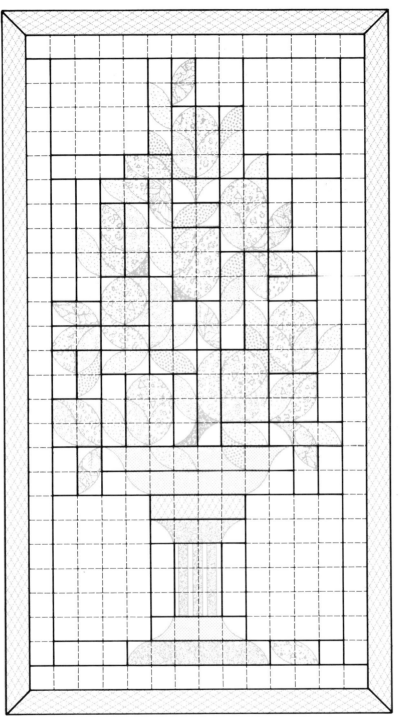

16 × 29 units

background, inserted a contrasting piping, a device I often use as an enriching detail.

You'll need four fabrics for the leaves and stems. For the rose petals select at least three; a few more add a lot more zest. You can substitute a special border stripe for the fluted column of the urn.

If the project seems too large to undertake, look at the photograph of Arnold Savage's variation (at the end of Section 4). Although sewn by his three-dimensional technique, it's a smaller version that you can adapt. With Arnold's consent, I've diagrammed a blank version of his framed bouquet in Section 4. You're invited to fill it with your own arrangement of patchwork.

Valley Camp

Valley Camp

Quilter: Nancy Drum
Design by the author
Suggested unit size: 1½"
Dimensions: 33" x 42"
Color plate 14

The first title for the landscape was *October Camp* because I thought of that season as a good time for displaying a variety of colors in the ground, bushes, trees and hills. When Nancy Drum chose the design, the name was changed, because camping to her meant summer. The decision to strip piece the large tree taxed both Nancy's and my inventory of greens. We gave ourselves more problems by choosing to break up the expanse of water. The bittersweet job of fabric selection continued over several weeks and into the hills. I didn't hear of

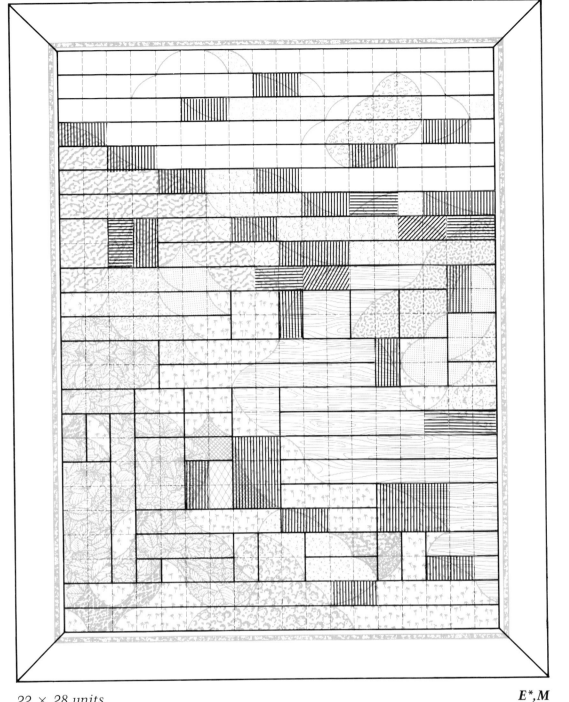

22 × 28 units   **E*,M**

any further problems, however, once Nancy began piecing her picture.

If you compare the illustration of *Valley Camp* to the color plate, you'll see how much simpler I've made the diagram. It still calls for five to seven fabrics for trees and shrubs and four or five for hills. But without internal patches in the large tree and river, you will have more area to emboss with quilting. Should you prefer the more

fractured look accomplished with extra fabrics, you can enlarge the picture in order to use bigger patches. It's not often a design can be enlarged without loss of appeal. The trick is to insert more internal interest as Nancy did.

Along with the original curves, you'll need templates for these elongated ones: 1½″ x 3″, 1½″ x 4½″ and 3″ x 4½″. The illustrated border is two units wide.

Della Robbia
Design by the author
Suggested unit size: 1½"
Dimensions: 15" x 42"

I have long intended to develop a design reminiscent of the elegant, fruited wreaths of Christmas. This draft, more like a frieze of fruit than a wreath, has six varieties of fruit tucked in among the leaves. Reading from the top down, you'll see a nut, lemon, peach, more nuts, a pear, plums and an apple. If you select a tan fabric for the nuts, that choice and other light colors for the lemon and peach will allow you to weight the wall hanging with heavier tones for the plums and apple near the bottom.

You can draw a template of a right triangle to help form the nuts, but it's easier to make a template that represents a whole nut. Start by drawing a 3″ square on template stock; draw markings for 1½" squares and, taking the 1½" concave template of the original curves, mark and cut off two opposite corners. These are the rounded edges of the nut. A patch cut with this template will make a more realistic nut with a dark line of embroidery going from one pointed corner to the other.

To establish a major division in the assembly plan, I divided the design vertically through the center. Thus it was necessary to divide some of the fruits and one leaf into separate modules. Organizing your patches, vertically if possible, will help you maintain a visual image. This is particulary important when piecing a module that doesn't develop into a familiar shape. In the next section read about a layout sheet for organizing patches.

The elongated curves of this design are 1½" x 3″.

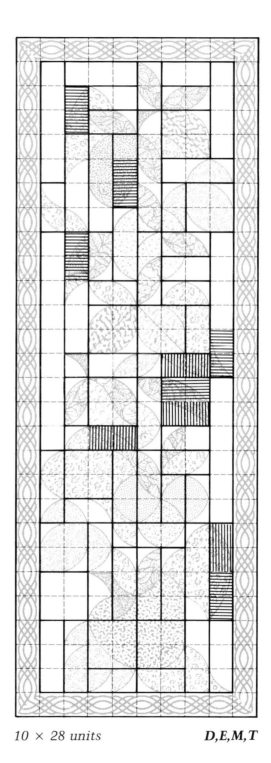

Della Robbia

10 × 28 units **D,E,M,T**

Sent With Love
Owned by Hazel Carter
Designed and quilted by the author
Unit size: 1"
Dimensions: 12" x 20"
Photo on front cover

Only about the size of two pillow tops, *Sent With Love* was my first wall hanging. I was delighted with its portability and brevity. Practical in size and simple to assemble, it was a pleasant change of pace from what I call a more serious work.

If you want to try the curves for the first time, this brief work is a good choice. At first the idea of 1" units may intimidate you, but most of the modules combine several curves into one patch. So you'll use the single curves mainly to finish modules into larger squares and rectangles.

The code letters overlap in meaning. The constructed curves are the double-scaled ones and vice versa. To construct the convex curves that are shaded in the working diagram, first copy the 1" and the 2" templates of the original curves. Place the 1" convex template on the corner of the 2" one to mark the rim-like template.

Because I'm so familiar with this short subject, I use it to illustrate some general tips in the next section: how to cut the constructed concave patch (refer to the bottom shaded square) from strip piecing and how to make a helpful chart for organizing the curves. And the little bird is the subject of several variations in Section 4.

This piece doesn't have a true border. Comparing the sketch with the color photo, you'll see that here I omitted only the corner appliques, merely scallops of the binding plus bits of color that fill in the corners.

Sent With Love

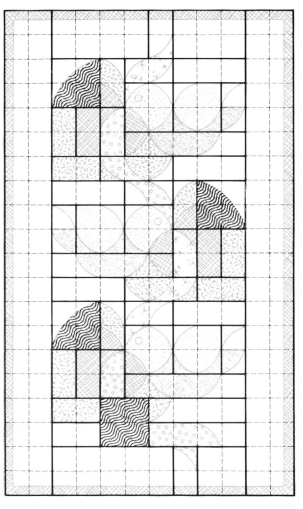

12 × 20 units   ***C,D,M***

Festooned Fleur-de-lis

Festooned Fleur-de-lis
Design by the author
Suggested unit size: 2"
Dimensions: 34" x 36"

With 16 leaves on each side of the Fleur-de-lis, I chose an assembly plan that lets you cut each one whole. Section 5 has the com-bination template for you. The simple leaf shape is one I use often, so I'm in the habit of piecing it into a rectangle by adding a concave curve at either end. Notice that the major divisions suggest assembling the central medallion first and then adding the side borders. The top and bottom borders are at-tached last.

17 × 18 units   *E*

You'll also see other practical combination patches to cut for this design. For instance, in the medallion there are two pairs of elongated curves on either side of the center vertical column. It's sensible to cut the design module on each side as one patch, which will have a concave edge and one that's convex.

Use two color-related fabrics for the cascading ribbon. The leaves can be a variety of tints and tones. Or choose only a medium and a light color to imitate the leaves of a Silver Maple tree when a breeze ruffles them enough to turn up their pale backs. In addition to the basic curves, you'll need templates for a set of elongated curves, 2″ x 4″.

Tettegouche Autumn
Designer and quilter: Rosemary Root
Unit size: 3½"
Dimensions: 49" x 63"
Color plate 16

Rosemary Root told me that the inspiration for her design came from an autumn trip along the north shore of Lake Superior and the Tettegouche *(tet-a-goo-che)* State Park just as the leaves had started to turn. The falling leaves of her quilt aren't pictorial, but the slightly cupped shapes swinging back and forth on their gentle descent create a clear impression of Indian summer. Rosemary's contribution is especially for those who prefer larger patches, two abstract blocks for repetition and plenty of leeway for fabric selection.

Once you've referred to the instructional diagrams on how to make the four necessary templates, look again at the partial quilt sketch. In the first column where blocks A, B, A touch, you'll see two possibilities for combination templates by using the concave curve in conjunction with the convex or with template C. (Template D remains single for leaf fabrics.) Making templates of the above combinations, actually the design's modules, will permit you to assemble columns with fewer seams. Take this short cut only if you choose quite stable fabrics with no tendency to stretch, because, with this method, you'll sew bias to bias for the entire length of the column.

The seven odd-numbered columns start with block A; the seven even-numbered, with block B reversed and alternating with block A reversed. Each column contains 18 blocks. You can add more for a full bed quilt or subtract for a smaller project.

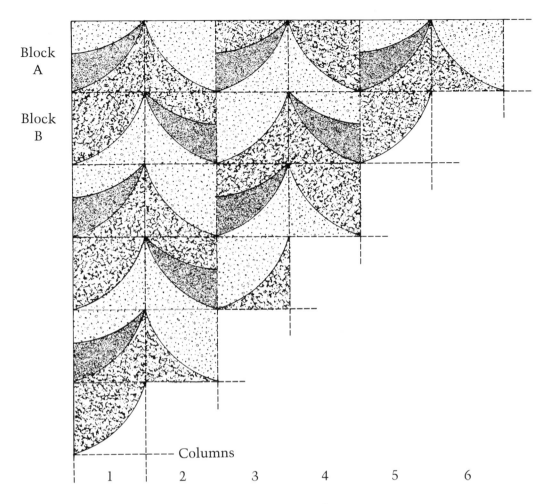

Block A

Block B

Columns

1 2 3 4 5 6

Partial assembly diagram for **Tettegouche Autumn.**

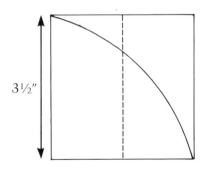

$3\frac{1}{2}''$

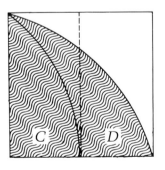

C D

For Block A Templates:

1. *Copy the 3½" templates of the original curves onto template material. (See Section 5.)*

2. *Draw a vertical line through the center of the square to create rectangles (as shown above).*

3. *Using a flexible curve as described in Section 1, draw the Curved Two-Patch arc in rectangle C.*

4. *The convex curve is now divided into two new templates, **C** and **D** (shaded areas).*

Imari Dragon

Imari Dragon

Designer and quilter: Jane Blair
One quarter of the original rendered by the author
Unit size: 1½"
Dimensions: 28½" x 30"
Color plate: 12

There are times when a patchwork idea seems to be a natural for the system's curves. Yet as the pattern takes shape, the designer becomes aware that certain areas call for different shaped curves and other patches, the necessity to take liberties, even to move beyond the curved system. Jane Blair had the confidence to do so for her

splendid pieced dragon quilt.

When Jane gave me permission to render her pattern for this book, I told her it would be a simplification. Even so, as you see in the working diagrams, there are still six units with constructed curves. But they're practical extensions of the Curved Two-Patch System, and most have been used elsewhere in this book. Start with the original templates in the correct size of square for three types of constructed curves and use a rectangle for the fourth. Reading from left to right, use a half-scale curve to finish marking the extra template in the first and second diagrams. See *Tettegouche Autumn*

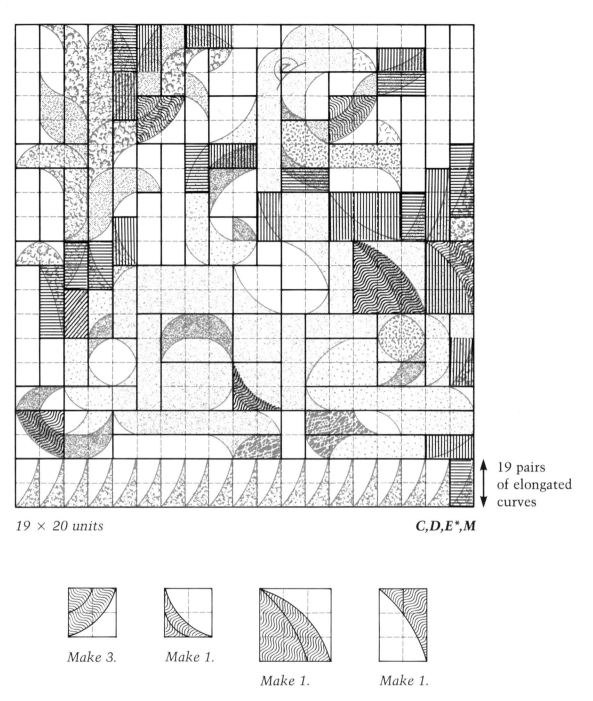

19 × 20 units   **C,D,E*,M**

19 pairs of elongated curves

Make 3.   *Make 1.*   *Make 1.*   *Make 1.*

Types and number of constructed curves.

to complete the third and Fig. 13 in the next section for strip piecing the fourth. Besides the above, make templates for the following sets of elongated curves: 1½″ x 3″, 1½″ x 4½″ and 3″ x 4½″.

To make a four-dragon quilt similar to Jane's, make two of the illustrated creature. Rotate one for the opposite corner. Then, with the pattern reversed, do the same for the other two corners.

Stacked Deck

Stacked Deck

Design by the author
Suggested unit size: 1½"
Dimensions: 33" x 27"

Stacked Deck is in the just-for-fun category, appropriate for the den or rec room or as a gift for a bridge player. Originally my intention was to draft a very simple wall hanging with the four aces, but nothing very exciting happened, not even when I added the smaller scale letters. Then I thought of using building blocks and stacking them. That prompted a more humorous title followed by the see-through blocks. In this plastic age, the motifs that appear to

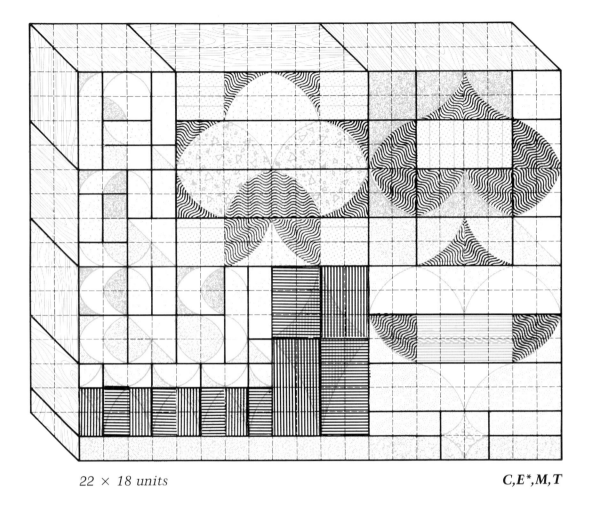

22 × 18 units   ***C,E*,M,T***

float could be on transparent fronts of some blocks.

For the heart, spade and the background of the club, strip piecing is suggested, but not obligatory. The drafted templates in the letter blocks are merely right triangles; however, there are parallelograms for the two borders, top and side. Save yourself some work: Make only the largest template, 3″ x 15″, and cut it down in size as necessary. (It must be reversed and used vertically for the patches in the border at the left.) You'll also need elongated curves in these sizes: 1½″ x 3″, 3″ x 4½″ and 3″ x 6″.

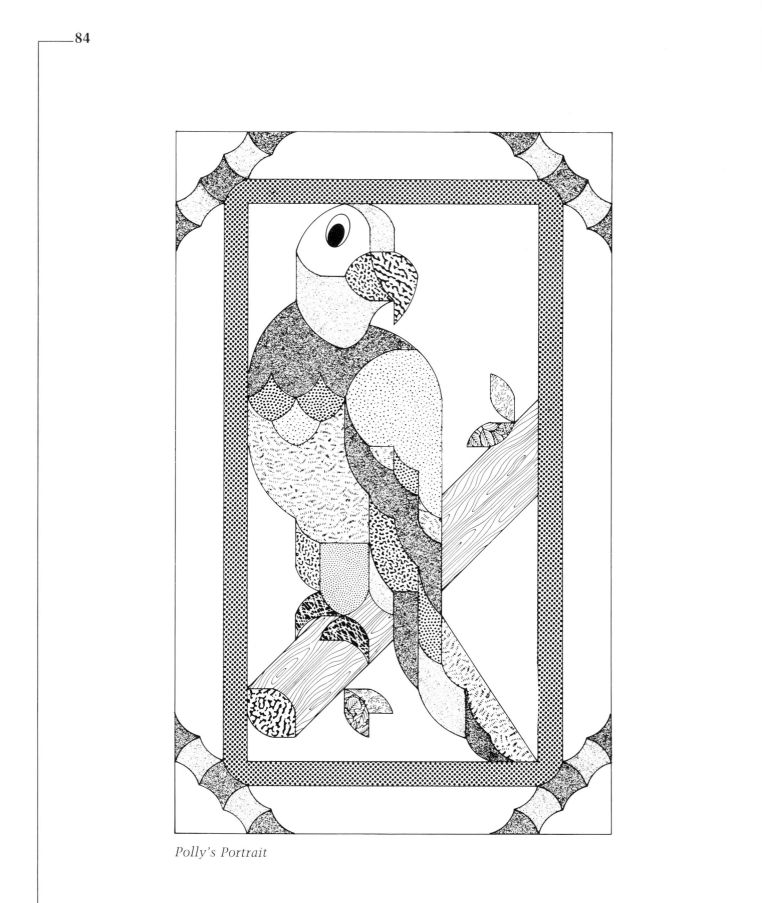

Polly's Portrait

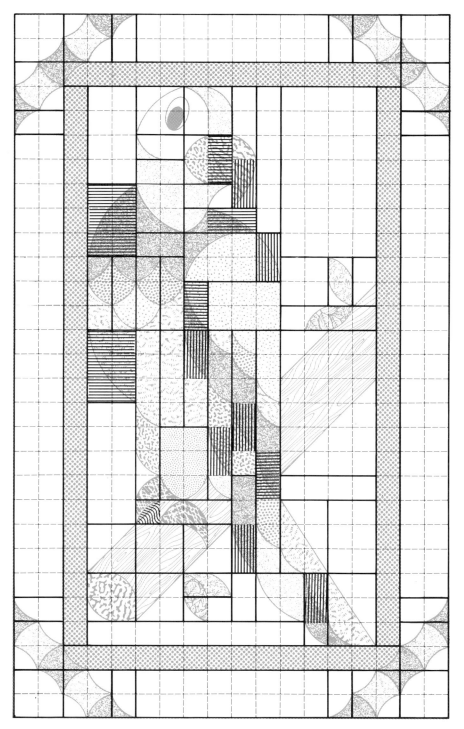

18 × 29 units   ***C,D,E*,M,T***

Polly's Portrait

Design by the author
Suggested unit size: 1½"
Dimensions: 27" x 43½"

Polly is for color. Reserve the bleached pastels and grayed calicoes for your next Victorian or country-style bed quilt. Here's an opportunity to dig into your supply of clear primary colors. With some judicious planning, you can manipulate four fabrics to cover all the feathers.

Besides the original set of curved templates, Polly calls for two sets of elongated curves: 1½" x 3" and 3" x 4½". The code letter T refers to shapes required to piece Polly's perch and her tail. The working diagram reveals that only squares and various sizes of triangles are necessary for most portions of the perch. The lower cross section of the branch can be constructed in the manner that I described for the nut in *Della Robbia*. In fact, you can use the same idea to obtain a pattern for the two segments of Polly's tail that fit into 2 x 3 units: Draw a rectangle, 3" x 4½", and bisect it diagonally into triangles. Place the 1½" concave template in a triangle's corner, mark and cut it off. The remaining shape is the template.

Notice the suggestion for the inner border is to overlap the sides with the top and bottom strips (1 x 14 units or 1½" x 21" plus seam allowances). If you develop the habit of making marks in the seam allowances to indicate units, lay the curved template on the strip to mark and cut the rounded ends, plus seam allowances of course. Join a concave patch of the bamboo to square off the border.

The bamboo segments make effective corner decorations, but they're deceptive. They tempt you to cut a patch for each segment of bamboo and to join the segments diagonally. Easy enough, but I avoid this approach because the next step entails sewing a series of concave patches to the scalloped edges of several convexes. I prefer to have more control of bias edges and to cut the corner blocks as illustrated. Some combinations are still possible, and the final seams are straight.

Constantinople

Designer and quilter: Rita Erickson
Pattern adapted by the author
Unit size: 1¾"
Dimensions: 59½" x 43¾"
Color plate 15

We all learned early in school that Istanbul was once called Constantinople. That earlier name seems to be a more fitting title for Rita Erickson's wall hanging. Constantinople evokes the romance of the ancient Byzantine Empire and the characteristic domes of its architecture.

The illustrated version is a simplification of the photographed quilt. As you can see in the assembly diagram, the design can be almost entirely pieced in strips. Although the sketch doesn't indicate that the water and the land are to be cut of various fabrics, it's an option. The quilt is a mixture of the basic curves in three sizes (1¾", 3½" and 5¼"), strips and some squares and triangles. Construction will be even easier if you applique the five constructed curves. You also have the choice of strip piecing or embroidering the windows.

What will demand time is the fabric selection for the tiers of buildings and towers. Particularly with pictorial subjects, you must try to get your work up on a vertical surface for viewing. Pin up your patches and take at least four giant steps away to judge whether a print is still apparent or if there's enough distinction between subtle shades.

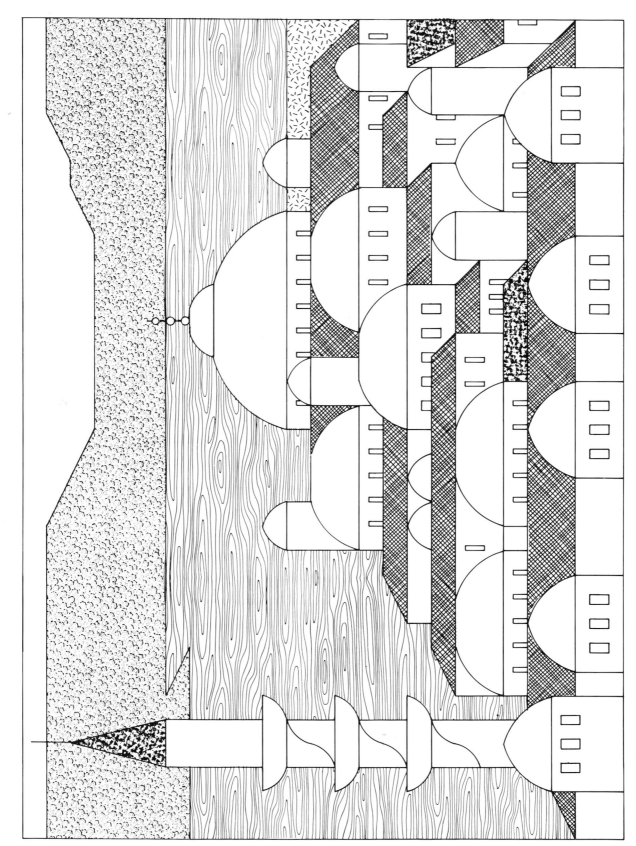

Constantinople

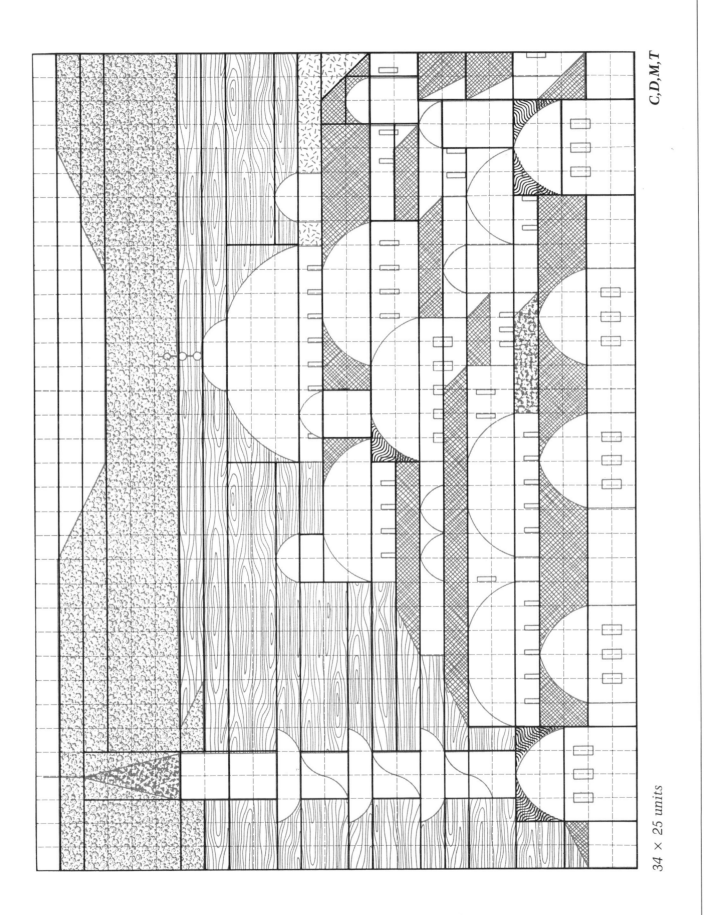

C,D,M,T

34 × 25 units

90

Tips, Thoughts and Quilters' Comments

SECTION THREE

*A Curved Two-Patch block
made by Esther Castano*

Tips and Thoughts

It's **unnecessary to enlarge a design** to full size for patterns, because you will trace the appropriate size of templates for the original pair of curves, the elongated ones and several curved combinations. This realization may take time to accept if you're accustomed to each patchwork pattern being printed with templates in a specific size. But to emphasize the point, I should tell you that I have never enlarged any of the Curved Two-Patch diagrams when I've made a project from them.

Redrafting is needed only when the assembly of a project indicates a template not printed here. (But I don't consider triangles cut from a square as a reason for a redraw.) For *Dragon Lair*, *Allegro* and *Sent With Love*, I simply chose the template sizes and assembled the projects by following a scaled diagram. It was only for the shapes of the books in the EPM logo on the title page that I redrew a portion of a design to full scale.

If you design your own projects, however, you may find a full-size drawing advantageous for other reasons. In a complex project where a maze of combination templates are possible, you can trace all from the full pattern. Also, some shapes that looked good in a small drawing may need to be refined. This can happen in a design containing elongated curves in long rectangles mixed with the more rounded ones forming squares; because the longer the rectangle, the more shallow the arc will be. A full-scale diagram may reveal that the arc in the rectangle should be deeper. An enlarged design, particularly a pictorial one, may tell you that to construct certain shapes with more realism you must go beyond the *Curved Two-Patch System* and draw a completely different curved patch.

For the simpler patterns in this book, those short on details, the decision to use small or large scale patches can make the difference between **miniaturization or elephantiasis**, between charm and ugliness. The pictorial motifs with curves work particularly well with smaller templates. Notice that several of the quilters, whose designs in this book deal with realism, based their work on 1½″ units. (That is not to say that all patches were of that size. A small scale can be offset with combinations. Although some modules must be finished with single curves, the combining of patches lets you work with larger fabric pieces most of the time.)

Often I mentally try out sizes for templates. When I've determined the amount of space a shape will cover, I try to relate it to an object nearby. For instance, if the size template I'm thinking of using will develop a kitten's head bigger than this sheet of paper, I'll scale down the size of template.

As a general rule-of-thumb, the larger the scale of patchwork, the more important details are. Think of the spectacle of a hot-air balloon enlivening the sky with its various colors and patterns. It wouldn't be as visually exciting if it were a massive ball of one solid color and no design details. I thought about this when I developed the balloon pattern that has curves to be strip pieced.

Relating the original pair of curved patches to a square of fabric makes it easier **to estimate yardage** needed for a project (Fig. 7). Let's say your design requires ten concave and ten convex curves of one fabric. If you use 3″ templates, you can cut one patch of each curve from a 4″ square of fabric. Theoretically, in an eighth yard of 45″ fabric, you

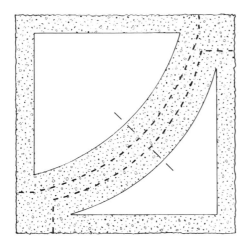

Fig. 7. *For yardage estimates, the two curves with seam allowances fit on a fabric square that is approximately 1" larger than the unit formed when the curves are sewn together.*

can cut ten 4" squares yielding all 20 patches. As an actual purchasing guide, the method must be tempered to allow for contingencies, such as patches that will not "nest" together in a compact shape. And making allowances for possible mistakes is wise too. For what quilter hasn't filled the quota of wrongly marked reversals? Estimates can also prove to be more adequate for larger projects than small ones. When the estimate for a bed quilt is based on how many patches a fourth yard will yield, sometimes a couple inches of fabric are left over in each and every quarter yard purchased. This is often enough for another row of patches. But, when you need only one quarter yard for a smaller project, cut just one patch wrong and you may be out of fabric and out of luck. One way to build in assurance against skimpy estimates is to figure each pair of curves as fitting on a larger-than-necessary fabric square.

For the elongated pair of curves, base the fabric estimate on a rectangle that allows for seams of both curves. Whether the long side of the rectangle is vertical or horizontal on the fabric will affect the amount of yardage to buy.

Over several years I've worked with every type of curved template I could think of, hoping to come to a defensible decision as to which is superior. But I can only say that each type has advantages and drawbacks. I've concluded that you must choose the type with which you're comfortable. Regardless of my preference, I've seen excellent work produced by all **three types of templates** illustrated in Fig. 8. (Although the sketches show only the original Curved Two-Patch pair, the templates vary in the same way for the elongated curves.)

The pair in Fig. 8a is usually referred to as hand-sewing templates. In my own work, I use this type exclusively, even though I do as much stitching by machine as I do by hand. These templates minus seam allowances have two advantages: The stitch line on the curve is marked—this is of paramount importance to me. Also, with these templates it's easy to construct combinations without having to subtract seam allowances from the interior of multiple forms. On the other hand, the pointed ends of the concave template can be irksome. It helps to premark fabric with parallel lines to establish the width of patches. To completely avoid using the skinny-pointed template, use the fatter convex one to mark the curve. The curve is the same on both templates! And you have the parallel stitch lines already drawn on the fabric to guide the placement of the template. Use the fatter template to mark not only the curve of the concave patch but also its vertical side. Think about it. Pour a cup of coffee, look at the illustration and read the last few sentences again.

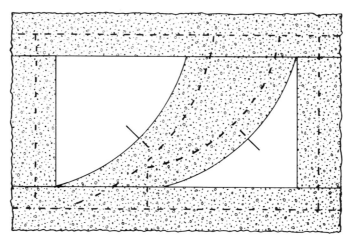

a. *These templates trace all of the stitch lines. They are shown on the wrong side of the fabric, which was premarked with solid lines to establish the width of the patches. Seam allowances (dash lines) are added to patches.*

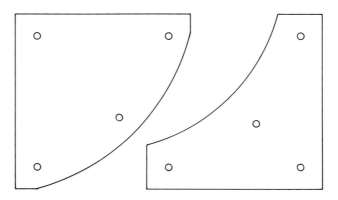

b. *This pair has all seam allowances included. Holes mark ends of the stitch lines and centers of the curves.*

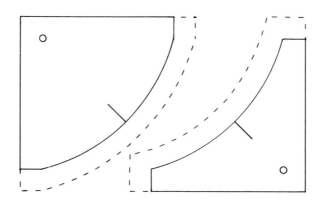

c. *The above templates mark the stitch line for the curves and the cutting lines for the other edges. Dash lines show the seam allowances to be added when patches are cut. Holes mark the corners where straight seams intersect.*

Fig. 8. *Three types of Curved Two-Patch templates.*

It's easy to see in Fig. 8b that one advantage of the templates for machine stitching is the concave one whose thin points are enclosed by seam allowances. For this set of templates, I've added holes to define the ends of the curved stitch line, its center and the corners where straight seams intersect. Some quilters use an eighth-inch paper punch to make perforations. I feel that such a practice permits the pencil to enter at an angle and mark inaccurately. I've made smaller holes by burning through plastic template stock with an electric stencil pen. I've also found it quite easy to punch holes in plastic with the pointed end of a compass. It's difficult, however, to see small pencil dots on many dark printed fabrics. Furthermore, this set is not convenient for making combinations.

Fig. 8c shows what I call half-and-half templates because half of the seam allowances are included and half are omitted. (Again I've added the hole that locates the intersection of the straight seams.) I like the fact that the curved stitch line is traceable. I also think the concave template of this set could be used as an alternate to the one in Fig. 8a, if you check the templates for accuracy and premark fabric in the manner described above. The disadvantage of this pair of templates is that its success depends on a reliable memory. I find it too easy sometimes to cut the ends of patches minus seam allowances.

Real quilters don't hide fabric. Such active inventory must be accessible.

The single curved templates, the originals or the elongated ones, can be combined into many shapes. Some occur so often in a design that you'll want to take advantage of their increased mass. Several common shapes are shown in Fig. 9a through 9e. (Three small sizes of these **combination templates** are printed in Section 5.) Figs. 9a, b and c illustrate different portions of a clamshell. I'm apt to cut up this shape whenever it's necessary for straight-seam assembly. You'll be surprised how often the leaf shape (Fig. 9d) lies undetected in a pattern as a module quite unrelated to plant life. To see examples, turn to the black and white photo of the numeral for Section 1. The wedge shape (Fig. 9e) also appears often. In fact, I probably use it as much as any combination form. In Figs. 9f and g, the shapes may not be as recognizable as a clamshell or circle, but they are practical as combinations. Look again at the last two figures. Can you see the bird's head of *Sent With Love* and the body of a fish?

I avoid some combinations, particularly scallops (Fig. 10a). Although the shape appears to be a practical combination, I prefer not to sew a patch with concave edges onto a convex dome. Instead, I make a double patch from the template shown in Fig. 10b. (Notice that it's identical to Fig. 9e.) Then I attach a concave and a convex patch above and below. I repeat the rectangular module in reverse and join the two vertically. For machine stitching, even with the matching of seams, I find this method easier than piecing whole scallops.

You'll notice that the sketches of the templates show a number of markings. They are bits of information to transfer to the seam allowances of patches. If you've worked with curves, you know that they are easier to match if you have some marks to guide you. That's the purpose of the dashes in the center of each curve. It's also

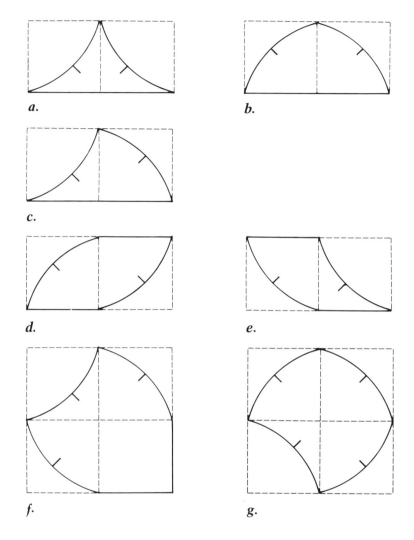

Fig. 9. Some curved combinations make practical templates. The above common shapes are printed with a dash grid to illustrate how they might appear in a diagram.

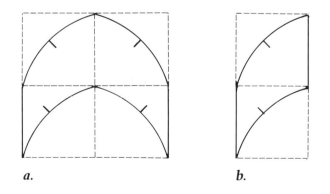

Fig. 10. Rather than use the curved combination of Fig. 10a, try the half scallop of Fig. 10b for easier seams.

helpful to have a mark in the seam allowance of combination patches to spotlight where the straight line ends and a curve begins. In Fig. 11, look at the top of the template where the convex curve starts its downward swing. If the mark in the seam allowance were not there to announce the change of direction, it would be difficult to tell exactly where the point of the concave patch (on the right side of the figure) must be pinned. One trial without the spot identified should convince you of the mark's value.

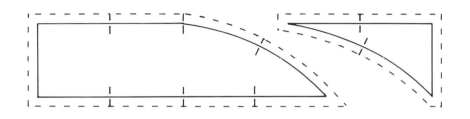

Fig. 11.   *Marks in the seam allowances of a combination patch are important aids for piecing.*

Many of the motifs and short subjects include strips of fabric with a curve at one end (Figs. 12a and b) or at both ends (Fig. 12c). Whenever the design has several strips (of variable lengths) with a curve at one end, and if the longest strip will fit on template stock, I make a pattern of it. After marking the longest strip of fabric, I cut from the template one or more units (marked with dashes) and trace the next shorter strip for a patch. The shortening of the template can be repeated as necessary. By marking fabric strips with a template, I'm less likely to miscalculate by just the width of a seam allowance.

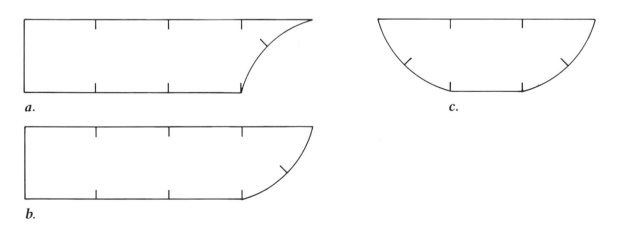

a.

b.

c.

Fig. 12.   *Templates for strips with a curve at one or both ends.*

When I choose not to make a special template for a strip with a curved end, I draw parallel stitch lines on the length of fabric and make dashes in the seam allowances in order to count the units in the strips. This method works well for constructed curves too (Fig. 13). With visible stitch lines and dashes marking the units of the pieced strip, I can accurately place the curved template on the fabric's wrong side. Before cutting, I make sure of three things:

1. I flipped the template over.

2. I placed it on the correct end of the strip. (On the wrong side of the fabric, the correct end is the reverse of the diagram.)

3. I've added the final stitch line and seam allowance only along the curved end. (It's all too natural for the hand, accustomed to marking completely around a pattern, to mark the vertical side of the curved template also and then sever the curve from the rest of the strip.)

To see where the strip of Fig. 13 is used, refer to *Sent With Love* in Section 2. It's the constructed curve that's part of the bottom heart and part background fabric.

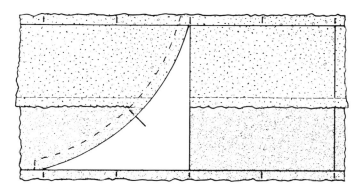

Fig. 13.   *Marking a constructed curve at the end of a pieced strip.*

I find it curious that many quilters who have made a Curved Two-Patch design will say that, because seams would be distracting, they combined curves even though it meant setting- in patches and a more complex assembly. I hope there are two ways of looking at this. I advocate combining patches whenever it's logical and makes work easier. Yet I feel there is a special **dimensionality in a quilt of curves** that is also embossed by a grid of seams. What's wrong with flaunting good craftsmanship? It seems to me that an architect does so in a building where he not only exposes the skeleton but also highlights it as decoration.

So much quilting lore and technique has now been recorded in books that it's possible to promote our craft as a branch of knowledge. Rather than "patchwork," we might call it "patchology."

Both Nancy Drum and Paula Libby discovered that a **reversed diagram** eliminates worry about forgetting to turn templates over on the wrong side of fabric. Because we constantly work with the wrong side of fabrics to mark, cut and sew patches, common sense says: Turn the diagram over to look like the work. Of course you can tape the diagram with the right side down to a light source (a window, lampshade or light box), but there's an easy way to reproduce the image in reverse. Remember before the days of copying machines when we used carbon paper? Do you recall mistakingly placing the carbon side up so that the copy ended up on the backside of your original? Do this deliberately to obtain a reversal of your design. Label it as such. Now as you refer to the reversed version to check the directions of templates on fabric, you duplicate what your eyes see and forget about mental gymnastics with flip-overs.

After a day of workshops in Illinois, Mary Jo Deysach and her husband took me out for a Chinese dinner. I still have the fortune-cookie philosophy from that evening: "She who says it can't be done is interrupted by she who is doing it." Has a feminist infiltrated the fortune-cookie factory?

In selecting fabrics for pictorial patchwork, you should rethink and maybe revise old habits. Intrinsically attractive colors and prints are generally the choices for a bed quilt. But when a project reaches toward realism, you need to step beyond the prettiness of fabric to create a mood or effect.

What you might consider ugly and would never choose for a bed cover or a garment could be perfect for a squirrel's shadowed hind leg, the inside of a cornucopia or the scar on a distant hill. Call this **a defense for homely fabric** if you like. And I know what homely is. My fabric collection is a repository for oddities. Nevertheless, I had the fabric for turquoise ripples of water and a camouflaged tent (see Nancy Drum's *Valley Camp*), a dragon's hot breath sputtering psychedelic bubbles (*Dragon Lair*) and the pages of a book (EPM logo). Should the occasion ever arise, I also have the fabric for a graffiti-covered billboard.

The quilters who deserve to be honored are those who teach the next generation to appreciate quilts and to keep the craft thriving for the coming century.

If your quilt project involves many fabrics and you're concerned about adequate variation of color value, consider **photocopying fabric samples**. Tape representative cuts to a sheet of paper, 8½" x 11", but take care to arrange the fabrics so they mimic their position in the quilt. With a black and white photocopy, you can make judgments without color overpowering your impressions. Esther Castano used this method for selecting fabrics for two of the section numerals. The idea may prevent disappointment when your quilt is hung in a dim corner of an exhibit and that soft rose appears indistinguishable from the beige background. The two fabrics were so complementary when you had them in your hands—six inches from your eyes!

In the first trial, the background of the striped apron is almost the same value as the fabric for the arm and the quilt's background.

Wanting to use black and white photography to show you what I'm talking about, I asked Nancy Moore if she would permit me to include photos of her first two trials with *Sunbonnet Sue, Herself*. She readily agreed. Having taught quilting, she under-

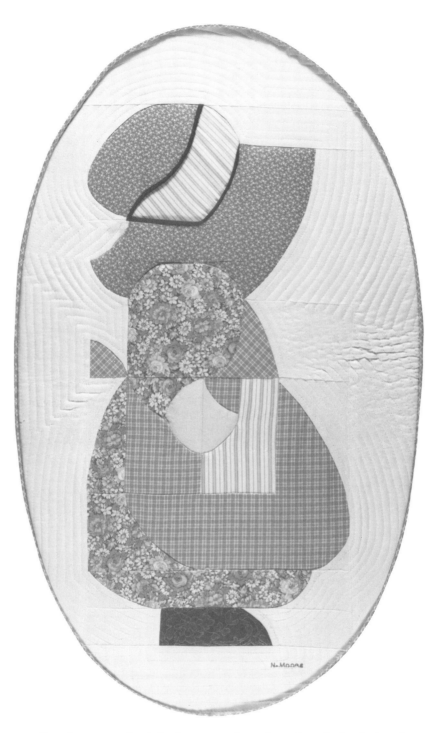

*For the second trial, the more densely colored check for the
apron helps define the arm and the apron tie, but the
printed and solid blacks (my suggestions) for the shoe and
hat trim overpower other subtle tones.*

stands that seeing examples of fabric selection is part of the learning experience. Look upon Nancy's experiments with fabric as learning trials. (See photos above and opposite.) Then refer to the back cover to see her final project.

At home we used wool comforters that Mother had pieced. We slept in unheated bedrooms and equated weight with warmth.

Almost any project will seem much simpler if you make yourself a visual aid, such as the **table for curves** in Fig. 14. It identifies what's merely inverted and what's reversed. Using the background fabric of *Sent With Love* as an example, the illustrated chart

tabulates not only the number of curved patches needed but also depicts the templates and how they look when inverted and reversed. (For this purpose the chart lists only the single curved patches necessary to complete the design modules of the project. Also required of the same fabric are several squares, rectangles, double-scale concaves and the constructed curve discussed earlier.)

A total of 23 concave patches of the background fabric must be cut, but only ten of them can be drawn with template A. Although some of these are inverted (rotated 180°) in the design diagram, you can draw a row of ten patches—all in the same direc-

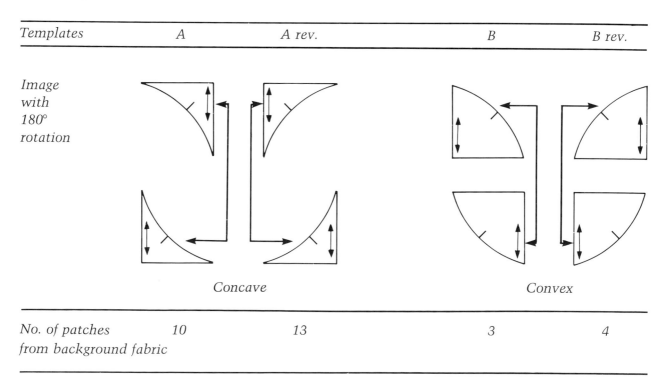

Short Subject: **Sent With Love**

Templates	A	A rev.	B	B rev.
Image with 180° rotation				
	Concave		Convex	
No. of patches from background fabric	10	13	3	4

Fig. 14. *A table to record the patches required of a given fabric helps identify what's reversed and calms the nerves.*

tion—without the grain of the fabric changing. Mind you, I'm talking about no change of fabric grain with patches inverted—turned from up to down, not sideways (which would be only a 90° rotation that does change fabric grain). I'm also assuming that you're not using a fabric with a nap, like corduroy, or some unusual print that, if inverted, would show feet in the air instead of on the ground. The other 13 concave curves of the design look like the illustrations under A rev. Therefore, you must reverse template A. Then draw all 13 patches to match one of the images under A rev. The convex patches are listed in the same manner.

In *Pleasures of Pattern* (New York: Van Nostrand Reinhold, 1982), William Justema states that repetition and variation are the principles of pattern. He says, "Variety is the intelligence of a pattern, what makes it worth noticing." If we pause to note the variation, we tend to remember it. It's like the often heard song, "The Twelve Days of Christmas." How many of us recall all the lyrics even though they're repeated 12 times? It's not the many lines of similar length and the same fast tempo that we remember. It's the shorter, sustained phrase, "Five go-ol-den rings." The change of pace gets our attention. In the same way, a bit of variety can punch up the design for a repeat-block quilt.

Many of the Curved Two-Patch motifs and short subjects are composed of only a few shapes—just curves, some squares and rectangles. It can be bewildering to see lots of curved patches turning in every direction.

Such visual confusion could cause you to abandon a project unless you use an easy way to organize the patchwork. I strongly recommend **a layout sheet** for this purpose.

Refer to the photo (p. 104) with the patches of *Spotted Pup* arranged on a flannel grid sheet. Your layout sheet can be even simpler. The unprinted side of a sheet of wrapping paper can serve as a good substitute. On it draw a grid of squares, each of which is equal to the size of your patches. (Don't worry about precision. This is only a visual organizer.) It's also helpful to pencil-in the curves by referring to the diagram. With this information in front of your eyes, you won't inadvertently rotate a sewn module when you replace it on the grid sheet. Look at the photo with a column of patches removed. See how little visual sense the isolated patches make? This may lead to a sewing error. If the grid sheet had the curves drawn in each square, you would immediately see that the unit 6B, although cut correctly, has been rotated 90° counterclockwise. (Use Fig. 15 as a reference.) Some of the patches in the isolated row

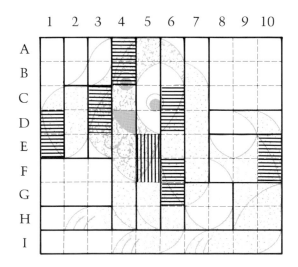

Fig. 15. *The assembly diagram for* **Spotted Pup** *charts the curves in rows and columns.*

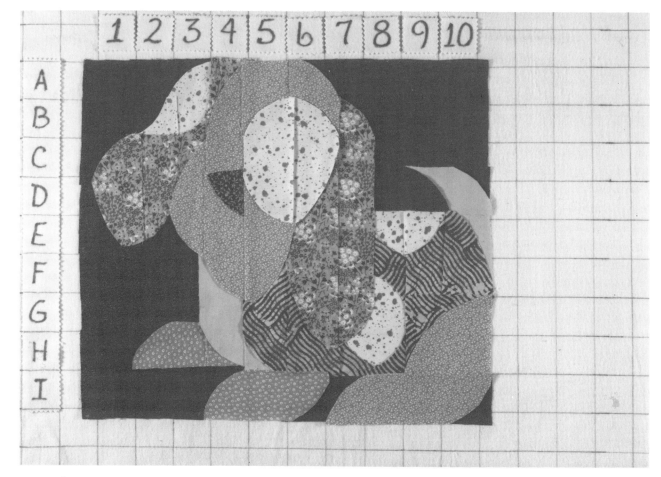

Spotted Pup

*The patches for **Spotted Pup** are organized on a flannel layout sheet marked with 1½" units. The outline of the pup is uneven because of overlapped seam allowances.*

were deliberately cut as single curves so that I could show you a rather subtle, but common, mistake and emphasize the importance of the layout sheet. But it's interesting to note that the more combination patches you cut, the less chance there is for mistakes.

Once a grid sheet is made, you'll check the placement and direction of the curved patches only one time. Then with the patches pinned in place, you can sew without constant doubts that inhibit relaxation and enjoyment. To have fun with curves, it takes just a little homework.

I wish "quilt" and "guilt" didn't look so much alike. They evoke emotions that I want to keep widely separated.

What's all this false pride about how few pins are needed to hold curved patches in alignment for sewing? Two hands are hardly enough to maintain the forced fit. That's **what pins are for**. Rather than have to rip out a bias seam, use pins aplenty.

Patches for column 6 A–H, are removed for sewing and shown at the right. What's wrong with their arrangement? Refer to Fig. 15 to find the mistake.

The answer is given in the text of "a layout sheet."

In a manufacturing process, accurate measurements of a product are not left to happenstance. Not only are the machinery and tools precision made, but product parts are inspected for quality control. Too often in patchwork we purchase precision templates and, with no further check on our work, pray that everything will turn out just fine. Fearing that my prayer might not be answered, I've learned to use **a blocking cloth for quality control**. This procedure not only checks the precision of my work but makes quilt assembly easier.

For some time I've been teaching the blocking of patchwork as a basic technique, one that has been largely overlooked. All of us were warned early that too much pressing could stretch our work, but the advice stopped there. Of course fabric gives under pressure, but seams can contract as well as stretch—like an accordian. Why not stabilize patchwork before pressing? We accept this logic when we block knitted articles, and we don't question the practice of blocking needlepoint. But in neither of those two crafts are exact dimensions as critical as in pieced quilts!

The easiest quilter to convince of the value of blocking patchwork is the one who has had the frustrating task of fitting the work of others into a quilt top. Often this entails tugging, tucking, maybe a zig or a zag and, most of all, diplomacy. If she hopes to keep her quilting friends, she says nothing but resolves never to be caught with an assembly job again. She has learned that precision patchwork can save assembly time.

Try to convince another quilter and she might smile and say, "Well, this quilt is just meant for my bed. Anyway, imperfections prove it's handmade." After her quilt is completed, she decides after all to display it on the living room wall. Or, with a belated rush of pride, she enters it in a local show or contest where its parallelogram shape distracts embarrassingly from its beauty.

The quilter who sells her work through shops can expect her work to be hung so as to spotlight any waviness of patchwork rows. Visitors, judges or potential buyers will take notice. If they don't, she can be sure that her own eyes will always be drawn to the imperfections.

I make various sizes and shapes of blocking cloths according to the type of patchwork quilt. If you're planning a quilt of repeated squares, only one blocking cloth is necessary. For this method you must have seam lines marked on patches. A practice I strongly recommend for curves. From a very firm fabric, such as sports cloth, cut a square somewhat larger than your patchwork. On this blocking cloth, draw a square equal to the desired size of a finished block. (The dimensions of the drawn square do not include the seam allowances of your test block.) It's wise to use a waterproof pen to draw the square. Form corners with a right triangle. (Without precision there's no purpose for this procedure.) Place the blocking cloth—with the outline up—on the heel of a thickly padded ironing board. Push pins into the blocking cloth around the outside of the outlined square and depress them into the padding. Any type of short pins works best, but don't use plastic-headed pins that might melt. On top of the blocking cloth, place the patchwork block wrong side up so that marked seam lines are visible. At each corner of the seam lines, pin through the patchwork, through the corner of the outline on the blocking cloth and into the ironing board pad. Again, completely depress the pins to facilitate pressing. In the same manner, add enough pins to hold the patchwork seam lines in alignment with the outline on the blocking cloth. If you've used accurate templates, marked and sewn your patches carefully, the patchwork will match the blocking cloth without your having to ease in excess fullness or stretch the fabrics. (If the block does not fit the cloth, review each step of your patchwork to find and correct the problem.) Press and allow to cool before removing pins. You now have a quilt block of precise measurements, one that you can reproduce with the exact same dimensions.

Real quilters don't have manicures—at least, not for long.

Whenever I see a quilting design marked with pencil, I want to climb into a pulpit and pass down an edict: If you must—I mean, actually feel compelled to—mark with a pencil, don't draw solid lines! Use stitch-length **dashes to mark quilting designs**. It's the same idea as the dotted lines on stamped embroidery patterns. Your quilting will cover most of the dashes, but a solid pencil line shows between each and every stitch.

Applying beeswax to thread not specifically made for quilting is a common practice. Still, it took **quilting with metallic thread** to make me realize I wasn't using the wax to my advantage. This type of thread, at least the one I like, consists of three coiled strands. Stiff and wiry, they don't stay together long enough to pass through the tiny eye of a quilting needle. I now wax metallic thread before cutting it from the spool. Then I cut within the waxed area so that the strands don't separate.

About the hostesses of an itinerant quilter: I never had one I didn't enjoy. Never was in a guest room without quilts. And never saw a closet that wasn't stuffed with project paraphernalia.

Intending to experiment more with machine quilting, I finally bought the **walking foot attachment** for my sewing machine. The new toy sat in its box until I finished a hand- quilted piece and was ready to bind it. Attaching binding, I admit, is not my favorite pastime. The length of bias I pin to a quilt's side is never right. In fact, I had stopped trying to use pins for holding the two in alignment. I know some quilters avoid a seam of so many layers by sewing the binding to the patchwork top before quilting. It was too late to do that now, and anyway, my quilt needed a firm seam to stabilize the edges. Since it's designed to handle bulk, I tried the walking foot attachment. Neither the binding nor the quilt's

edge creeped, crawled, stretched or bunched. What a joy!

Quilt addiction isn't a new malady. I was told that when Grandma wanted to quilt at night, Grandpa would hold the lantern closer so she could thread her needle.

At times I have reasons beyond impatience for **finishing a project without binding**. For *Allegro* I wanted the waves of color to run down and spill over the lower edges. (See color plate 1.) A narrow binding would have looked too inadequate to stem the flow. Also, the border fabric that some of the patchwork waves pass over has a narrow stripe that I chose as the final edge of the top and a print following that stripe which I didn't want to show even on the back of the quilt. So I had one reason not to make a binding and another for not turning the front over the back. I decided to turn in both sides. Not a new idea, but an old one with a small variation. I turned under and pinned the seam allowance of the quilt top. Next I trimmed the batt to match the top's edge. I allowed extra width for the quilt lining so I could fold it over the batt. By compressing the batting just a bit, I kept the back slightly shorter than the front, maybe by an eighth of an inch, and whipstitched the back to the top's folded edge. Because the narrow rim of the top is available for the final hand stitching and the quilt back is slightly shorter, the edge doesn't reveal stitches on the front of the quilt, and the back can't roll over and appear where it's not wanted.

Do you have a copy of *The Curved Two-Patch System* or *Curves Unlimited* and need a **substitute for a lost Block Marker**? Wherever supplies for draftsmen and engineers are carried you can buy translucent drafting paper in various grid sizes. The see-through grid works for either book. There's also a similar template plastic with a ¼″ grid called Lam-i-graphs™. You'll find it easy enough to determine the curves illustrated in a ½″ scale, but you'll have to mark other divisions in each square of the plastic grid sheet to see smaller units. If you are concerned about losing your Block Marker, make a pocket holder for it like the ones in library books. Simply cut off an end of a business-size envelope and glue the pocket to the inside of the bookcover.

Before I took an interest in this craft, I sent my oldest off to college with an old quilt instead of a good wool blanket, which would surely be stained, moth eaten and generally ruined. He reported on a home visit, "Mom, no matter how I put that quilt on my bed, it doesn't fit." So I relented and purchased a blanket. Years later, I learned that the quilt had been hand- pieced in the late 1800s by one of my husband's great-greats. Nobody sleeps under our prized antique now.

Fig. 16 illustrates the back of a dress yoke from a Simplicity pattern of a few years

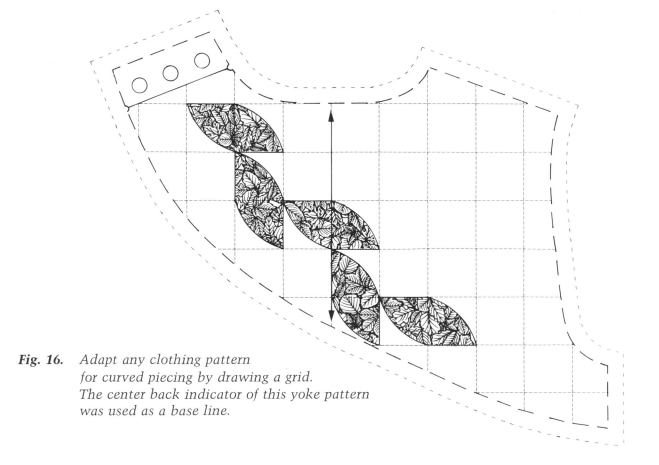

Fig. 16. *Adapt any clothing pattern for curved piecing by drawing a grid. The center back indicator of this yoke pattern was used as a base line.*

ago. Even though the yoke is asymmetrical, the sketch shows how easy it is **to adapt a clothing pattern for curved piecing**. Using the center back (see arrows) as a base line, I drew a 1½″ grid on the yoke pattern. Then I played with designs. I decided on a cascade of simple leaves and asked Ruth Him to make the pieced dress for me. She made a template for the leaf and assembled the yoke in jigsaw fashion. You can experiment on any pattern piece. I suggest starting with a ½″ grid so you can try ideas in various scales before deciding on the final size of the curved patches.

By using a garment as the background, it's easy to place a patchwork design. This photo shows pieced and embroidered balloons appliqued to a child's over-sized sweat shirt made by Joyce Buchberger. McCall's pattern.

Overheard at the Quilt National exhibit: "It's easy to spot the quilter. That's the one who stands almost against the work to check out the craftsmanship. Others stand back for the visual impact."

Many quilters know that museum people use **Orvus W A Paste**®, a Procter and Gamble product, to launder antique textiles. You may have wondered where to purchase this very mild, synthetic detergent (sodium lauryl sulfate, the base of many shampoos). Did you know it's sold along with horse-grooming supplies? A company spokesman told me that it's also purchased, repackaged and sold by some craft shops for cleaning needlepoint. It's labeled as an industrial product, not for home use. And, indeed, curators do not recommend it for your washing machine. With agitation, it's a high sudser. But I've used Orvus for hand washing. If you have means other than a clothes washer for laundering a quilt and you choose to try this product, use only one tablespoon to five or six gallons of warm water. (Orvus can coagulate in cold water.) Then use lots of water—and time—to rinse your quilt. Incidentally, it comes in 7½ pound containers, so divide with friends. Tell them they can "put it up" in mayonnaise jars.

Are you planning a trip by air and hoping to do some patchwork on the plane? Don't try to go **through airport security with scissors** that measure more than 4″ from the screw to the tips of the blades. They will be taken away from you.

There's one advantage to having an empty nest. My quilts finally have their own room. I had been worried by seeing how quickly my new quilts with man-made batting were developing permanent creases. Now all are spread out on pushed-together twin beds in a closed-off and darkened room. I read somewhere that quilts of the past may have survived because of such a practice. But I haven't continued the old custom of peeling off layer after layer and expecting trapped guests to admire each one. Probably because the bed underneath would still have to be made.

I have a lovely needlepoint pincushion that I received as a gift. I can't bear to throw it away, but it's no longer useful because my quilting needles rust in it. Quilt shop owner, Zoritza Matkowsky, tells me this won't happen with **a pincushion filled with hair**. You antique buffs who own a hair saver used by past generations can put your collectible back into service.

Quilters' Comments

Because a mere listing of the quilters who have contributed to this book would be little more than a bare-bone acknowledgment of their work, I asked them for a few words about themselves, their backgrounds, style or working methods. Most quiltmakers consider pen-and-paper work a waste of good quilting time. They would rather let their quilt projects speak for them. But all kindly responded and allowed me to choose a few personal tidbits to speak for them on these pages.

Nancy Ashley of Maine wrote, "I'm a would-be artist. I studied calligraphy, dabbled in graphics and ad layout and dreamed of going to art school before I discovered quilting. For me, this is an ideal medium, tactually as well as visually satisfying. Although I've helped to plan hundreds of quilts— for others and myself—at my 'gourmet fabric shop,' I seldom have the time to make the ones I design for myself."

Jane Blair, a professional quilt artist from Pennsylvania whose works have appeared frequently in Quilter's Newsletter Magazine, has devoted a regular eight-hour day to quilting for 17 years. "I'm interested in innovative design and color, but still want the end result to be more pleasing to the eye than shocking to the soul." About her work in this book she added, "The idea of Imari Dragon just grew from a tiny picture of a Chinese figurine—something clicked with the curves."

Suzanne Brown, a Kansas quilter who was her state's winner in the Great American Quilt Contest, 1986, said, "I've always done something with my hands, from knitting to huck "weaving" (embroidery on huck toweling). I began as an applique quilter and have progressed to piecing on the machine. My style changes with the quilt."

Joyce Buchberger of Arizona, formerly a professional seamstress, now stacks the mending in her quilt room until the kids outgrow it. She wrote, "It took me almost a year to feel comfortable about taking over the living room for my quilting." Then Joyce made another admission. "I've always loved all forms of needleart, except one. I once paid to get out of a knitting class."

Esther Castano is a quilter from New York who has worked extensively with the Curved Two-Patch System. "Quilting satisfies many of the senses. The feel of the fabric. The joyful sight of color. Sometimes just transforming a scribbled design into a piece of fabric art gives me a sense of power and amazement. I keep returning to the two-patch curves to help satisfy my insatiable interest in design."

Claudia Coyle of New York started quilting ten years ago without help from know-how books or workshops. She used her quilted pieces to coordinate what she called "Grandma's-attic decor." She admitted, "I used a Turkish towel as the filler in my first project and actually quilted through it." She also remarked, "The curves are a perfect answer to my frustration with painting and appliqueing pictorial images."

Susy Davis teaches quilting in rural New Zealand. Although she often feels "cut off" from the main quilting groups of her country and finds access to fabrics quite difficult, she has exhibited nationally and attended the Continental Quilting Congress in Virginia. "I see my isolation and rural environment as a plus in many ways. I would like my quilts to have a real New Zealand flavour as that is what's all around me."

Patricia Dolan, a water colorist from Pennsylvania, now combines the techniques of painting and quilting. "Rarely do I keep my original quilt design intact. Sometimes the angles look dreadful in full-size projects. But knowledge of the media's limitations frees me to explore finishing touches, such as beadwork or painting. My work reflects who I am—a complex being, interested in the intricate details of life while keeping an eye on the whole of it."

Nancy Drum of New York is a mechanical engineer turned quilter. She wrote regarding her work in this book. "Valley Camp reminds me of many happy backpacking trips in the Adirondack region. For this bit of pieced scenery, I chose a small scale because there is almost no wall space in our new contemporary home. In order to hang and enjoy my pieces, they have to be small. Besides, engineers can't multiply without a calculator. With the 1" scale, I only had to count the units!"

Rita Erickson of New Jersey wrote about her quilt Constantinople. "When I first saw the photograph that I used as the basis of my quilt, the domes immediately suggested the Curved Two-Patch System. I placed the domes, minaret and building shapes on a grid and 'imagined' their details. The result is neither a literal interpretation nor pure fantasy, but something in between. I have a whole file of photographs waiting to be interpreted in fabric."

Karen Flanscha of Iowa has been actively teaching quilting to groups in her state since 1980 and, among a long list of credits, she served a term as president of the Iowa Quilters Guild, Inc. Quite naturally the pieced version of her state guild's logo, which appears in this book, appealed to her. She added, "I'm not only a self-taught quilter, but in reverse of the usual tradition, I've taught my grandmother to quilt."

Janet Gillespie of New York, a fourth generation quilter, stated, "One of my fondest memories is of sleeping at Grandma's house on a feather bed with quilts on top." She also added, "I enjoy machine piecing, but I mark my fabrics the same as for hand piecing. I feel this gives me accuracy. I have one rule: I'll unpick and resew a seam three times. Then, no matter what, it stays."

Ruth Him of New York is an accomplished seamstress as well as a quilter. Recently she has become a partner in a quilt shop and helped form the New York-Pennsylvania Quilters' Consortium. She talked about her start in quilting. "When the Bicentennial came along, I decided there should be some quilts for my brother's children. And there was no one in our family doing that. Since then, there have been many baby quilts."

Sheri Hughes. another past president of the Iowa Quilters Guild, Inc., belongs to four different guilds. She wrote, "I enjoy the challenge of piecing a Curved Two-Patch design. It's like putting together a puzzle. I lay out small designs on a gridded rotary cutting mat. For larger designs, I draw a grid with a water-erasable pen on a bed sheet, which I hang on the wall."

Jean Jackson is from Minnesota, but in the winter packs up her quilting and heads for Arizona. While many prefer either patchwork or applique, Jean is a crossover quilter. "I find applique to be the easier, but I occasionally combine it with curved piecing." Jean mentioned another interest. "After being asked to demonstrate quilting to grade school children, I became interested in quilt history and now share that knowledge with other groups."

Jean V. Johnson, formerly from New Jersey and now from Kansas, is a popular national quilt instructor well-known for her strip-pieced pictorials. "Incorporating the Curved Two- Patch with my strip piecing adds a natural look that's difficult to achieve with straight and angled cuts alone. It's a natural extension to my way of designing." Referring to her design variations that require fewer Sandpipers, Jean added, "These are for the person who, after piecing one or two birds, has absolutely 'had it.'"

Paula Libby of Maine, an N.Q.A. certified teacher, included in her biography, "At the age of five, I was encouraged to play with my grandmother's sewing machine. Now, living in a coastal fishing village with my husband, son, five cats and a dog, I look forward to settling in during the cold winter months and to quilting. My favorite pastime is designing and piecing intricate designs. The more complex, the more fun!"

Nancy Moore of New York and her husband have a sewing machine sales and service shop. A self-taught quilter with expertise on the machine, Nancy was still hesitant to try Sunbonnet Sue, Herself in curved patchwork. The hesitancy didn't last. She made three! Each time she made templates of stiff Pellon®, combined more patches, tried various printed fabrics and experimented with several styles of machine quilting. As she put it, "I love finding short cuts that give the same professional finish."

Jeannette Muir of New Jersey has taken workshops with many quilt artists, all of whom suggested developing "your own style." Jeannette wrote, "Well, my style might be called 'Alphabet Soup' (Avery, Beyer, Crow, Diggs, etc.), but I'm still searching for identity in 'I.' I feel creative, but I frequently need inspiration from rugs, floors, math and science periodicals."

Faye Quayle of New Zealand, when on a visit to London in 1980, came across the book **Discovering Patchwork**. "And I really did discover patchwork. Since then I've been able to attend two quilt symposiums in the USA. I'm fascinated by the design possibilities of Seminole patchwork, curved seams and tessellations and the impact of Sashiko quilting. I see everything around me in patchwork. I long to create my environment with my needle."

Rosemary Root, another quilter from Minnesota, said, "The women in my mother's family have all been quilters, back to my great-great grandmother. Most of my recent quilts use gradations of color. I like to combine two or three color groups ranging from light to dark in various combinations. Although the Curved Two-Patch is only one of the techniques I use, I especially like the sense of movement the curves provide."

Arnold Savage of Ohio became interested in quilts when he attended the 1933 Century of Progress quilt show in Chicago. He said, "I've had the 'quilt pox' since that time." Having a fine collection of ancestral quilts has probably fanned his interest. He's the originator of The Three-Dimensional Piecework System, a technique used in Bouquet for Joyce. When I exclaimed about the hours of labor in this work, he replied, "Eight hundred hours isn't much. I have one quilt that took me over 30 years to complete."

Dot Stutter of British Columbia, Canada stated, "I did my first patchwork while sitting on the school steps waiting for Mother to return from her job at the war plant. I was 7 or 8." After Dot's children were born, she sewed professionally. "I've also done lots of theatre and costume design. For The King and I, I made sure Anna's bed had a patchwork quilt. I like to play with quilt design. I've made many small Curved Two-Patch projects and have a drawer full of curved designs."

Joan Thunell of Minnesota talked about her new quilt group that call themselves "Committed Blockheads." Everyone makes 20 one-of-a-kind quilt blocks, one for each member. "This method eliminates tedious duplication for the person who wants a repeat-block quilt." Then Joan added a personal note. "Quilting is a friend; I'm never lonely or alone because I have so many projects. If I feel like piecing, there's always a block to join."

Maxine Townsend, a quilter from Maryland, recalled from her past, "I helped my mother make two or three quilts back in the early Thirties. Almost all the ladies in our small Missouri town quilted. But Mother refused to ruin her hands. The tops were sent out to be quilted. The entire quilt, fabrics and quilting, cost about $15. I never thought about quilts again until a 1973 local quilt show. Until then I was painting portraits. I no longer do anything but quilts and clothing."

Beverly Tremblay of New Hampshire described her quilting style as "investigative." She continued, "I'm always trying new styles and techniques. The closest I've ever come to doing a quilt series is a couple of different basket designs for a class I teach. I love a challenge and much prefer designing my own pieces. Still, my work tends to have a traditional feel."

Audrey Waite of Arizona is married to an Air Force career man. Her interest in quilting is as varied as the places where she's lived. "While living in Virgina, I did volunteer work at the Smithsonian's Division of Textiles and saw the need for quilters to learn about conservation. I began teaching quilting in Germany. I still teach and lecture on quilt collecting. My collection, which started with a family member's quilt tops, has become a link to my ancestral history."

Virginia Walton, a quiltmaker living in Ohio at the present and the wife of another Air Force career man, has found quilting to be a mobile profession, a means of easy transition into a new community. "I piece and quilt both traditional and original patterns on the sewing machine. There's something soothing in handling fabric. Sort of a tactile connection with the nerve center. Quilting, much like a backrub, releases tension."

Variations on a Theme

SECTION FOUR

*A Curved Two-Patch block
made by Esther Castano*

Most of the illustrations in this section are based on designs or photographs that you've seen earlier in this book. The various paper trials are to show you—if you haven't already discovered—that fun and surprises come with grid play. Lessons learned while I wasn't even trying have often been of special value to me. I have also found that ideas can't be time-pressured. (It's no wonder so few quilters will subject themselves to the scheduled hours of design workshops!) It simply doesn't work to think, today I've got to come up with a good idea. Eventually I also learned that one idea usually holds the seed of another. I now know that I need to continue each investigation until I'm excited about my paper trial. As I once heard Dr. Linus Pauling say in a television interview, "You can't have good ideas unless you have lots of ideas."

Variations Within a Curved Motif

One of the easiest ways to play with design variations is to select a simple motif and confine yourself to internal changes. Essentially tell yourself that your personal detailing will be done within the block, which you expect to repeat for a quilt. At least you're not trying to be creative with all aspects of the project at the same time. And you can always change your mind later as the theme develops. This is the investigative process I used for *Dragon Lair*. (See color plate 11.) Fig. 17a shows a Curved Two- Patch rendition of a Yin and Yang block. If you think of each unit of the grid as a 2" (or larger) square, the design is too lacking in details. I tried varying the block by three methods, two of which are illustrated: adding straight-sided patches (Figs. 17b,c,d) and extra curved ones (Figs. 17e,f,g,h). I omitted the third method in which changes overrode the integrity of the original design. For my quilt, I chose to work with repeats of Fig. 17c and to intermingle stripped, L-shaped pieces with curved patches. I saw the design as the absurdity of trying to fit a square peg into a round hole and became absorbed in pitting the two elements against each other. During trials of block arrangement, the L-shapes kept leading outwards and suggesting a continuation. So I inserted the lattice work. From that point the Oriental theme was set; and it seemed quite natural to select a fabric with printed dragons, uneven prairie points as dragon teeth, gold metallic fabric for flames, etc. Yet, the entire quilt, even the theme, began as a trial, the internal additions to a simple block.

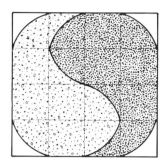

a.

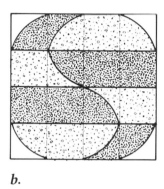

b.

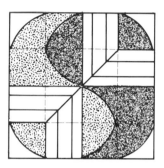

c.

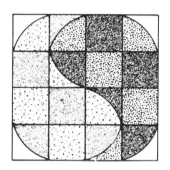

d.

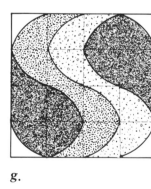

e.

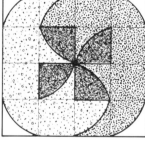

f.

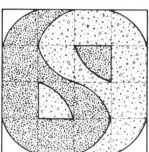

g.

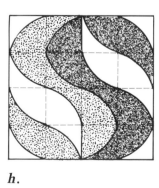

h.

Fig. 17. *A Yin and Yang design with variations in which the original design is still discernible.*

*Four center blocks of **Dragon Lair** made by the author. Along with 2" basic curves, the Yin and Yang blocks incorporate strip piecing and dragon-teeth points.*

To show you other ideas combined with the Yin and Yang block, I asked two other quilters to make projects by adding or altering the patches in the motif. (See the photographs opposite this page.) Audrey Waite chose to superimpose a checkerboard on the block (Fig. 17d). There can't be two design elements more incongruous than curves and a checkerboard, but the very fact that the combination is unexpected draws the viewer's attention. Jeannette Muir didn't develop her project with internal additions. She "blacked out" some areas, blended together portions of touching Yin and Yang blocks and, at the same time, extended other modules into columns for a linear design.

Linger-here Garden, Suzhou, China, 47" × 63". Designed and made by Audrey Waite. Multi-colored florals coordinated with solids. Machine-quilted.

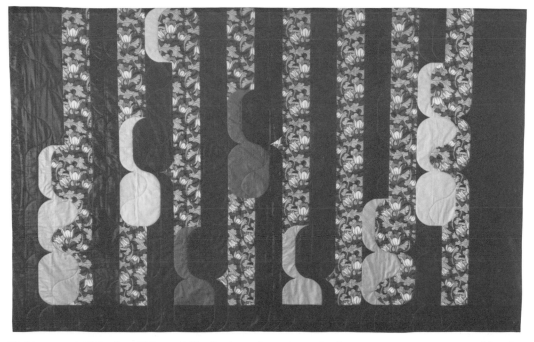

Tulips and Triads, 48" × 76", designed and made by Jeannette Muir. In black, mauve and beige. Machine-quilted.

If seeing a number of changes within the Yin and Yang illustrations has given you some ideas, take the set of seven variations to a photocopying machine to make duplicates for personal use. You'll save yourself an extra trip if you also make a set of reversed blocks before you go. Place a clean sheet of paper on top of carbon paper, which must have the carbon side turned up against the clean sheet. Now place the pair (with the clean sheet on top) behind the illustrations and trace with a hard lead pencil. The reversals will be on the back of the inserted paper. Mark each with "R" to distinguish the reversed drawings from the originals. After making and cutting apart copies of both sets, you can experiment with repeats of a single Yin and Yang variation, numerous combinations or some of your own variations.

Among the pictorial motifs of Section 2, there are a number of subjects you can modify by adding or substituting details. The *Patchwork Balloon* has a substantial area of straight-edged patchwork that you can redesign. The pig might be turned into a bank with appliques for a slot and partial coin. And Fig. 18 shows *Theodore* with patchwork variations reflected in his wardrobe.

Adding, modifying and substituting details are all part of the same idea to enrich and personalize patchwork. This is the purpose of suggesting the constructed curves in approximately a dozen motifs. Remember, even though a constructed curve adds an extra step to your work, it gives you a chance to use larger curved templates. Enhancing an enlargement of a simple motif

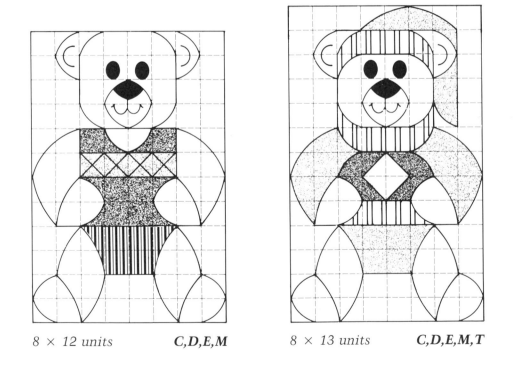

| 8 × 12 units | **C,D,E,M** | 8 × 13 units | **C,D,E,M,T** |

Fig. 18.   *Theodore with wardrobe changes. While the body shape remains the same, each figure has an area for strip piecing. Compare the substituted patches with the original design in Section 2.*

can seldom be overdone. Here are more suggestions for constructing curves and adding other pieced details.

> **Alphabet letters**: *Strips of uneven wedges.*
>
> **Stacked cars** *(later in this section)*: *Entire background of checkerboard patches.*
>
> **Frog**: *Water of horizontal strips.*
>
> **Giraffe**: *Spots cut from crazy piecing.*
>
> **Iowa Quilters Guild logo**: *Silo of brickwork patches.*
>
> **Hatched chick**: *Shell cut from crazy piecing.*
>
> **Sunbonnet Sue**: *Apron of checkerboard patches.*
>
> **Turtle**: *Shell cut from pieced hexagons.*

Paper Trials for Project Variations

Let me show you how I expanded a stylized bird motif (Fig. 19) into a quilted project. Starting with an obvious approach, Fig. 20a develops the motif into a block of 5 x 5 units. I added some background design suggestive of a board fence and placed it asymmetrically in the block to see what would happen when the design is repeated and rotated (Fig. 20b). Had I wanted to make a quilt with this repeated block, I would have continued adding blocks until I had 16 forming a larger square, because still other secondary patterns will emerge. But I was already curious about changing the position of one fence board (Fig. 20c). Now when four blocks are rotated, the boards line up and will continue to do so with more repeats (Fig. 20d). There will still be variations of the background shapes when

more blocks are added, but they won't be as dramatic as in the first trial. At this point, I put both ideas aside, because the birds appeared to be impaled on fences. I wanted something more cheerful.

For the third trial, I discarded the straight lines of the fences and inserted a ribbon in the bird's beak (Fig. 21a). Again I tried the rotation of four blocks (Fig. 21b). This produced an interesting shape in the center but odd negative spaces at the sides. By reversing the blocks in opposite corners (Fig. 21c), I organized the background areas to accept a filler motif. This helped distract the eye and led to the center where I turned the ribbons inwards and added a diamond for weight. The resulting background hearts were also welcome.

All four trials used the bird as a subject for a quilt block. I thought the next step should be to play with the motif as a border (Fig. 22). Using the shorter, original motif, 5 x 3 units, I paired the birds in Pennsylvania Dutch style. More than one pair per side seemed superfluous, so the border dimensions were settled with the addition of 3 x 3 units for corners. Once more I had too much uninteresting space in the border. This time I drew straight lines to appear like a banded border with birds fluttering in front of it. You can see I started my schematic drawing backwards, from the outside to the center, to make a special border work. I had to continue inwards and find a suitable medallion. I had enclosed 10 x 10 units and, theoretically, could use the entire space; however, I wanted some breathing space between the major design elements. To leave a one-unit rim that repeated the border bands would be tiresome, so I decided the center design should be only 6 x 6 units. From my first book, I chose a symmetrical floral design to contrast with the birds' shapes. The design

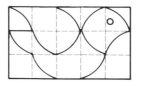

Fig. 19. *The bird motif from* **Sent With Love**
is isolated as a design module, 5 × 3 units.

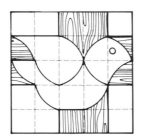

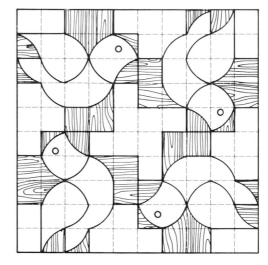

a. *A block of
5 × 5 units.
A board fence
design fills in
some back-
ground space.*

b. *A trial with rotations of block a.*

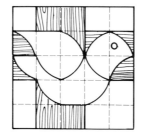

c. *Vertical col-
umn is moved
to the left.*

d. *A trial with block c and its repo-
sitioned background design.*

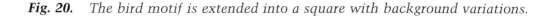

Fig. 20. *The bird motif is extended into a square with background variations.*

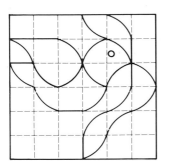

a. *A larger block, 6 × 6 units, with a flowing ribbon added.*

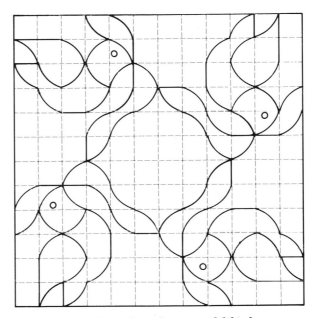

b. *The third trial with rotated blocks.*

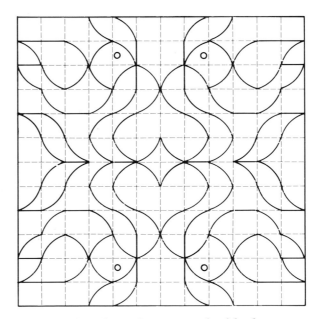

c. *The fourth trial reverses the blocks in opposite corners and adds filler motifs.*

Fig. 21. *The third and fourth trials use extra curved patches for additional interest.*

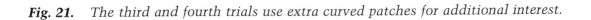

Fig. 22. *The number of units, 5 × 3, in the original bird motif determined the border dimensions. The overall design contains 16 × 16 units.*

modules remained so isolated from each other that I borrowed the heart and diamond from the last trial to tie all the elements together.

In the midst of my doodling with birds, ribbons and hearts, I thought of the Victorian valentines that often depicted a dove as the messenger. For this variation I wanted a single design motif. No repetitions. I tucked a small heart under the bird's neck and let the ribbons flow over it. The inner portion of the heart in Fig. 23 only widened the design. To add height, I added a rim (which involves a constructed curve). The problem was finding a border. A sentimental valentine needs one. Most were too heavy or un-interesting until I broke one corner of a simple, scalloped border to extend a rose bud and leaves into the background, sort of Art Nouveau style.

After all the paper play, it came time to put my patches where my pen was. I elected to make the little messenger and his sentiment in triplicate. (See Section 2 for the piecing diagram and the front cover.) I fitted the birds, flying in opposite directions, into a long rectangle, the shape I prefer for a small project. I know those birds aren't going to get anywhere until they decide to fly in formation, but I wanted to evoke a smile, not serious contemplation. (Turn to the title page for Section 5 to see a photo of yet another small project with the bird.)

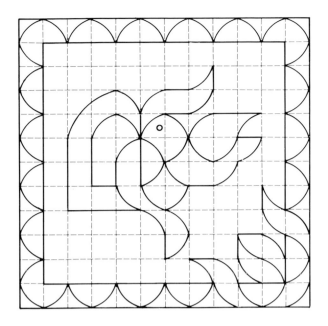

Fig. 23. *A postal valentine with the bird as the messenger, 12 × 12 units.*

Fig. 24 is the result of fitting two motifs into a small quilted hanging. In the original design, 8 x 8 units, the kitten tilts its head to see a ball at its feet. I thought I could add some comic tension by replacing the ball with a fish in a bowl. I drew one of the *Feeding Fish* on tracing paper and, following a graph-paper grid, outlined a bowl to accommodate its tenant. When I located this new motif below the kitten's head, I was disappointed. Too much of the kitten was covered. The bowl's ultimate position replaces only a few of the kitten's curves but doesn't interrupt any. Then to fill the empty space where the ball once was, I added squares to suggest a tablecloth. You quilters who have a baby quilt to make can find other whimsical combinations. Try the mouse near the sleeping cat. (See the color plate of Paula Libby's story quilt.) Or, if you're prepared to be a storyteller, put the mouse in front of an elephant, who's reported to be frightened of a rodent; or near the lion, who's grateful for the mouse having removed a thorn.

Sent With Love, *12″ × 20″, designed and made by the author after doodling on a grid.*

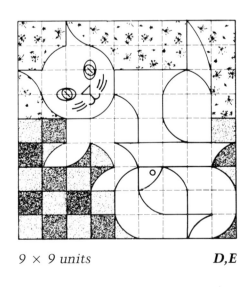

9 × 9 units   **D,E**

Fig. 24. *A paper trial combining two curved motifs.*

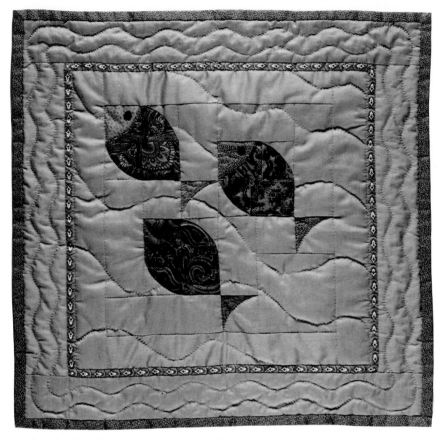

School of Fish, *20″ square, a fisherman's block made by Esther Castano. Pieced with the basic curves and bordered with various fabric strips.*

Short Subjects: Various Purposes

The one feature of short quilted subjects that so often distinguishes them from bed quilts is the border. Because the vertical drops of a functional quilt must cover the sides of a bed, quite a large area, the borders usually need a considerable amount of pattern. Short subjects, if they are going to hang on the wall, can be treated as posters, banners or pictures. If frames are needed at all, they are usually simple or subdued to let the viewer focus on the subject.

Keeping that in mind will shorten the time you spend on lesser projects. With the addition of a band or two for frames, it's possible to make simple, attractive articles from the motifs in Section 2 as opposed to de-signing complex works.

Is there someone dwelling in your house who could be called a car-crazy, teen-age male? Here's a project with easy borders that help develop the theme. *Demoliton Derby Star* (opposite) combines four pieced blocks and two bands of checkerboard patches. No corners to miter. Just add vertical strips to the sides and the quilt top is done. Then turn the front to the back for an easy edge finish. If you're worried that your work won't survive in the teenager's environment and if he's more interested in graphic effect than in workmanship, both of you may be more comfortable with a true banner. Forget the piecing and quilting. Instead, glue bright felt patches of the design modules to a solid piece of felt for the background.

Pillow with appliqued owl, a school mascot, made by Nancy Ashley. The embellishments refer to her son, a lacrosse player who's headed for Bowdoin College. Satinstitch embroidery and machine quilting.

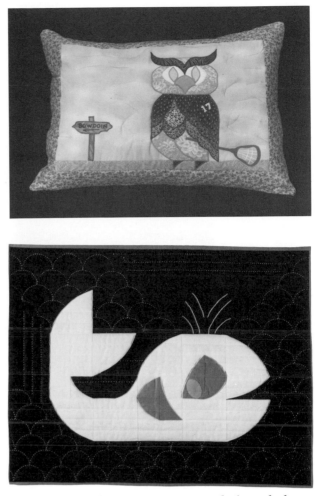

Flight of Fantasy, *39" × 47", designed and made by Claudia Coyle. Pieced with various sizes of the basic and elongated curves and framed with border strips. White, gray and shades of blue. Hand-quilted.*

Whale of a Tale, *28" × 22", a quilt for a baby pram by Faye Quayle. The whale, with a jade fin and an eye of pink and blue, is pieced with 2" and 4" curves. Sashiko quilting in the navy blue ocean. The batting is wool.*

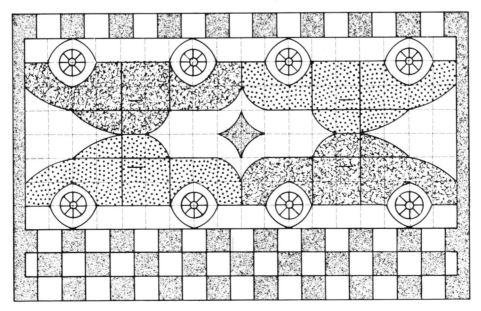

Demolition Derby Star, *19 × 12 units*   **D,E**

12 × 23 units   **E,M**

A door decoration

If there's a special little girl starting to show interest in your quilting, a room or door decoration of *Sunbonnet Sue, Herself* is a project on which the two of you can collaborate. (See diagram.) Let her choose the fabrics for the dress, apron and hat. You can fill in with other choices to coordinate the colors. Use as many combination patches as feasible without complicating assembly by machine. This will yield larger modules which she can help place on a layout sheet and bring to you as you need them. The immediate gratification of seeing the picture take shape on the wall will help sustain her interest. It's expecting too much of a child to appreciate the gift of a quilt when she didn't participate in its making. Why not show her some substitutes for the name "Sue." Her initials or a pair of traditional blocks, like schoolhouses. Perhaps she would like small floral blocks from *The Curved Two-Patch System*. Draw the final, full-size design on paper so she can color it while you sew the patches.

When I developed the diagram of the *Quilt Bee*, I was thinking of guilds who might want a patchwork logo. Is your group fairly small? Wouldn't it be fun to have each guild member represented by a donated fabric patch either for the scrap quilt behind the bee or for another portion of the logo? I leave it to you to figure out the ways and means of such a project. Or use the design, minus initials, as a block in a group-made quilt to indicate the project was put together during a typical quilting bee. With a change of initials the design is also adaptable for a quilt shop or individual. (See the photo of Joan Thunell's interpretation.)

12 × 15 units   **C,D,E**

A guild logo

Quilt Bee, 16½″ × 25½″, a studio sign with 1½″ curves by Joan Thunnell. The bee, spool and scrap quilt are pieced and appliqued to the background. The lower portion of the hanging is entirely pieced. Honeycomb quilting is by hand.

Quilters are a curious lot. They'll work long hours for months on a special quilt only to give it away as soon as it's finished. Their generosity is seldom equaled. But don't ask them to share the space where they work or store their fabric. I know a quilter who fusses because, in one of two large closets stuffed with fabric, her husband keeps a skinny fishing rod! If you need to give your family a notice of special occupancy, make a sign to hang on the door of your workroom. Or on the wall above your sewing machine or chest of drawers. *Number One* is for the quilter with lots of self-confidence. *Mine* is for the assertive. I'm sure you can find a reason to give away the *Number One* banner, but *Mine* doesn't transfer title so easily. Try another acceptable four-letter word. Both studio signs of basic Curved Two Patch are super easy to construct. I'm not talking about a piece for posterity here, merely a touch of comic relief. A respite from your masterpiece.

13 × 18½ units   **M**

Number One, *A studio sign*

12 × 12 units

Mine, *A notice of ownership*

A quilter's tote bag, 17" × 12" (approx. 43 × 31 cm.), by Suzy Davis. The Suffolk breed of sheep are black until they mature. Then their bodies become white. The pieced lamb and sheep are appliqued to a background representing the green hills of New Zealand. Hand-quilted.

Mentioning the generosity of quilters leads me to Jean Johnson. I had asked if she would design some kind of article as an easy, short-term project with curves, one intended for a specific purpose. She sent two! In Fig. 25, you see Jean's variations on a theme, developed much like the process illustrated in the earlier subsection, "Paper Trials for Project Variations." Borrowing the Sanderling from her bell pull, Jean used it as the subject for the table runners. (The sketches show one half of each. The dash lines across the tops indicate the centers of the runners.) In the bell pull, a wavelike shape represents the water's edge. The wave

becomes a continuous ribbon in the table runners. Jean offers two sizes: one for apartment dwellers and the other for those with longer dining tables. I think the short version might serve as a dresser scarf too. Don't worry about the smaller one appearing asymmetrical with a ribbon ending on one side. When you make the other half, another ribbon end will counterbalance it. I have not shaded the elongated curves because I want you to see the ribbons without distraction. However, you'll find more construction details with the Sanderling in Section 2.

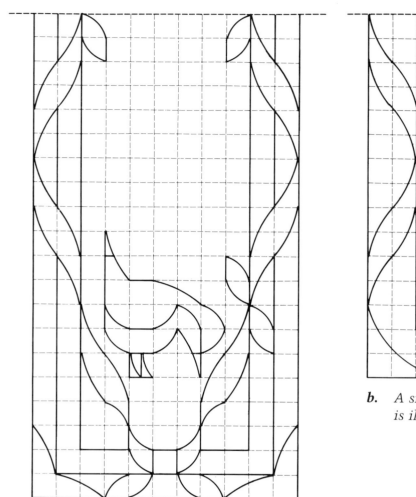

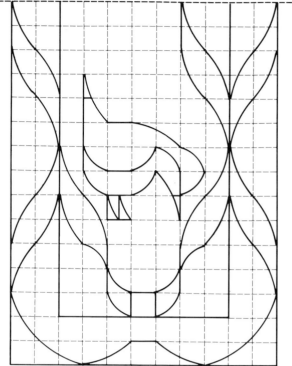

b. *A smaller runner, 30" × 11". One half is illustrated.*

a. *One half of a 40" × 11" runner.*

Fig. 25. *Jean V. Johnson's variations on a theme. Two table runners feature the shorebird of **Sanderlings, A Bell Pull.***

Pirating Your Own Projects

You haven't committed a crime if you rob from yourself. If a design feature you used in an earlier quilt still appeals to you, use it again. There's no guarantee that it will be anything more than a rehash, but still, the very fact that the idea comes to mind attests to its versatility and effectiveness.

Back in the Seventies, I designed a quilt with Mickey Mouse as the subject. What could be more natural than putting him in a movie? We quilters have borrowed ideas from all the related arts. I'm astonished that we've overlooked the potentials of the film strip. As a design device for a sampler quilt, it integrates dissimilar blocks that otherwise, even with color coordination, refuse to come together. Moreover, the movie setting is well within the technical experience of most quilters. Even the newcomer's introduction to the craft is typically a sampler quilt course. How easy it would be to

Mickey Mouse Movie, 48″ × 57″, appliqued, embroidered and hand-quilted by Peggy Spies in 1980.
A new sampler quilt with blocks of curved piecing (Fig. 26) borrows the framework of this movie.

Reel One: Ted & Friends
Dimensions: 48" × 58½"

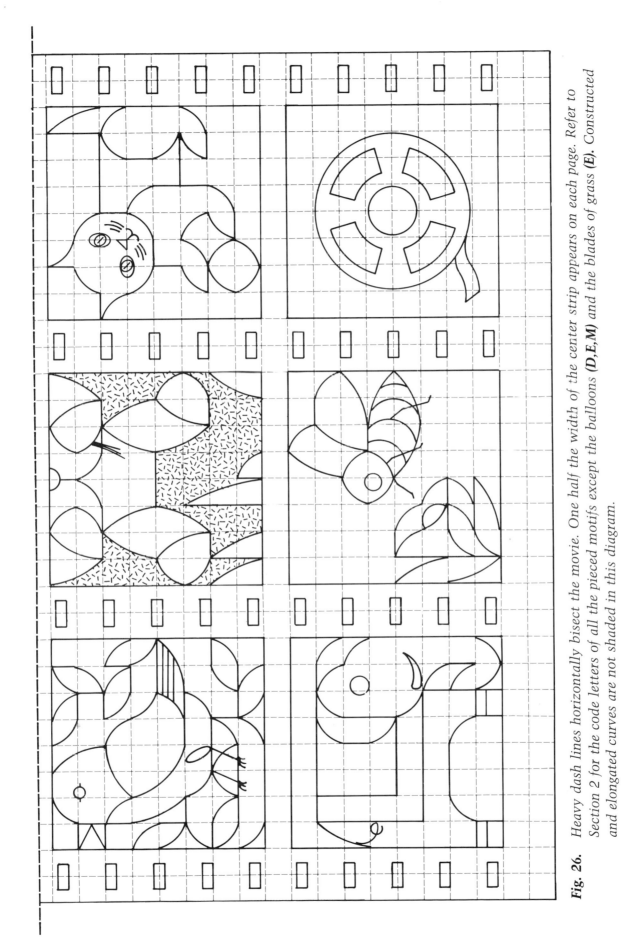

Fig. 26. Heavy dash lines horizontally bisect the movie. One half the width of the center strip appears on each page. Refer to Section 2 for the code letters of all the pieced motifs except the balloons (**D,E,M**) and the blades of grass (**E**). Constructed and elongated curves are not shaded in this diagram.

have the reels (they're identical, just inverted) serve as the applique lesson and the sprocket holes as an example of strip piecing. Each of the remaining blocks, taught as a different patchwork technique, becomes one frame of the movie. How about a movie of your favorite floral blocks? This could include both applique and Curved Two-Patch designs. For a more specialized theme, choose only rose patterns. There is an abundance of such patterns to be made by various techniques.

I have continued to be intrigued with the parallel between the quilter who selects and assembles blocks for storytelling or a graphic effect and the film editor who splices together the best sequences for plot development or visual impact. So much so that I pirated my own design of several years ago to direct a new movie (Fig. 26) in which each frame of the film is a Curved Two-Patch block. The result is more like a collection of favorite subjects than the sequential story of Mickey's day. Most of the motifs I adapted from Section 2 so they would fit into 12″ squares. The movie reels, though, are still appliques. (See Section 5 for the patterns.) Notice that the horizontal strips separating each frame of the film are deliberately narrower than the verticals. This is to give a general impression of images in fast-forward succession and to maintain a close visual relationship between the three frames of *Theodore*, who has been divided by the camera panning downward. The movie quilt isn't totally realistic, because I omitted two columns of sprocket holes. The middle film strip would normally have a complete set of its own. I took this license to keep the width of the quilt reasonable for a wall hanging. The vertical design of this quilt would not drape attractively on a bed, so I recommend that you resist the temptation to increase its size for that purpose. The quilt is named for its

star, *Theodore*, but you can personalize the design with a set of initials.

As the central figure for another possible movie sampler, Fig. 27 charts a three-frame panel of the giraffe. I don't take diabolical pleasure in cutting up animals, but the legendary length of his neck makes him an obvious choice. He's not the star of the previous movie quilt because he's based on a smaller scale than the other subjects. If you want to produce a new movie with this central character, it's best to base all companion frames on the same scale, 1″ units. Otherwise, the bird of the original movie, pieced with 1½″ units, will look like a pterodactyl of prehistoric times and overpower the giraffe. Notice that some compromises were necessary with the giraffe, although at first glance he may appear identical to the motif in Section 2. The brush of the tail is now embroidered rather than pieced. Also, the curve on the back of the neck is shorter. This means the hapless giant is bisected, not anatomically correct, but visually so.

Design Modules for Your Variations

The design modules in Fig. 28 are for your experiments. The new border *Coiled Ribbon* is a variation of the ribbon patterns in my two earlier books. This one differs because it has four triangles per block (Fig. 28a), if you cut them as separate patches for two corners. If, instead, you make combination templates, four patches in each block will have one edge forming a 45° angle. The corner of the border (above the block diagram) couldn't be simpler, just two large triangles. Experiment with drawing this border design on graph paper. Don't forget to reverse the directions of the blocks at the center of each side. The paper trial will show you the shapes formed in the centers when reversed modules meet. Classic in appearance, the new border will combine with many patchwork designs. *Fresh Blooms in a Basket* of Section 2 would be a good companion motif.

I also thought you might enjoy making a small wall hanging in the shape of Arnold Savage's project. With his consent, I've reproduced his unusual frame shape and added an interior dash grid. For each corner, use one constructed curved patch (Fig. 28b) with two patches of the combination (Fig. 28c). Remember you need to invert one of the latter. (See Section 5 for the combination template.) Adjust the size of the frame by adding or subtracting units in the straight sides of the border. In this way, you can fit the frame to almost any design, whether it's long and narrow or short and wide. Without any adjustments, the frame will accommodate a design of 12 x 12 units. The corners of the design will merely touch the interior of the frame's curves. Incidentally, the fourth trial with the bird motif of this section is 12 x 12 units. A single bird block, 6 x 6 units, tells us that any patchwork pattern of that size—repeated three more times—will fit inside the border as it appears here.

In addition, I've isolated the container Arnold used for his floral arrangement (Fig. 28d). Fill it with fresh fruit from Section 2 or with your own choice of flowers and leaves from *The Curved Two-Patch System*. Trace the bowl onto graph paper and experiment with design modules until you're satisfied. Then mark off the perimeters of your design for simple borders.

Fig. 27. *Three frames of a revised giraffe (opposite) can be the focus of an original patchwork movie. All 12″ companion blocks should be based on 1″ units. Rectangles of elongated curves are not shaded in this diagram.*

Bouquet for Joyce, *16″ × 20″, is Arnold Savage's three-dimensional patchwork interpretation of* **A Dozen Plus.** *Veined leaves were created with ³⁄₈″ strips sewn in log cabin fashion. (Photograph from Arnold Savage)*

It's been said that motivation follows action. When orchestrating the curved patches becomes playtime without pressure, exciting possibilities will move you.

You'll have a succession of ideas. Play with one and up pops another. And so on. And so on.

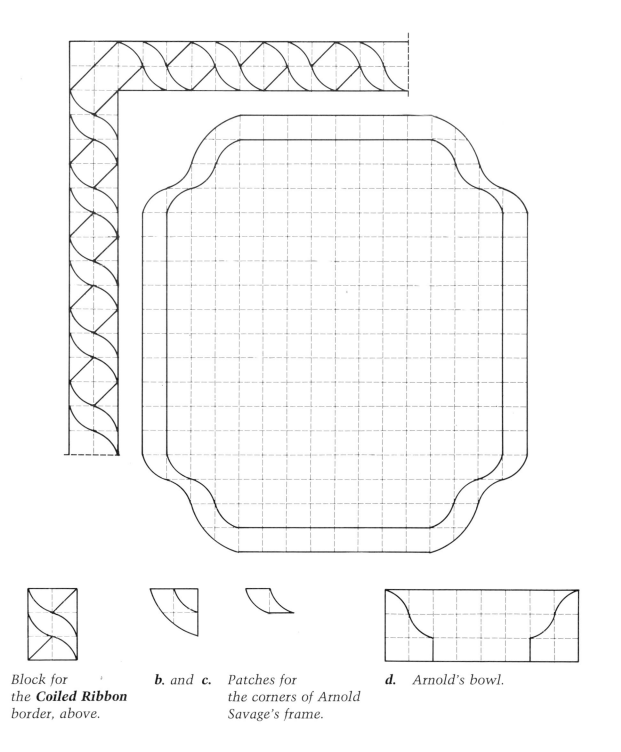

a. Block for the **Coiled Ribbon** border, above.

b. and *c.* Patches for the corners of Arnold Savage's frame.

d. Arnold's bowl.

Fig. 28. *A new border, frame and bowl for your variations.*

140

Templates

SECTION FIVE

*A Curved Two-Patch block
made by Jean Jackson*

Do you see the numeral in the patchwork photographed
above? Try turning the book at an angle so that the
lower right corner points to you.

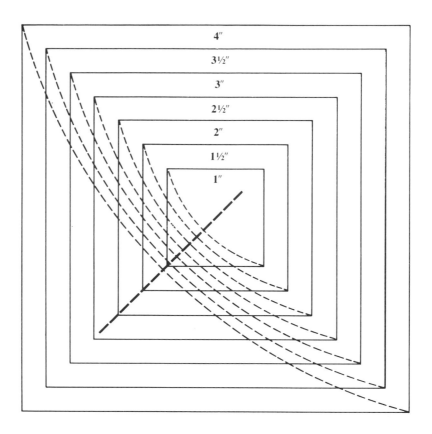

Basic Templates

Although the smaller templates are recommended for this book's motifs, here are seven sizes of the basic set for versatility in personal designs. Use these templates, printed without seam allowances, to form combination patterns.

An arc (the fine dash line) divides each square into the curved templates. The heavy dash line across the arcs is an aid in matching the curved patches. Copy this line on each curved template and later in the seam allowances of patches. Cut the three templates—convex, concave and square—of the size you need. Then check for accuracy. The convex and concave curves must fit together and be equal to the square.

Tip: It's easier to trace a smooth curve if you use short dashes.

Arc of the Basic Curves

The arc of the curves that form a square is drafted with a compass. No matter what size templates you use, the arc will always be of the same depth. This method for drafting the arc, established in *Curves Unlimited*, remains the same.

In case you need to draft a size not given on this page of templates, refer to Fig. 29 and follow the instructions below. Let's use 2¼" templates as an example:

1. Draw a 2¼" square on paper.

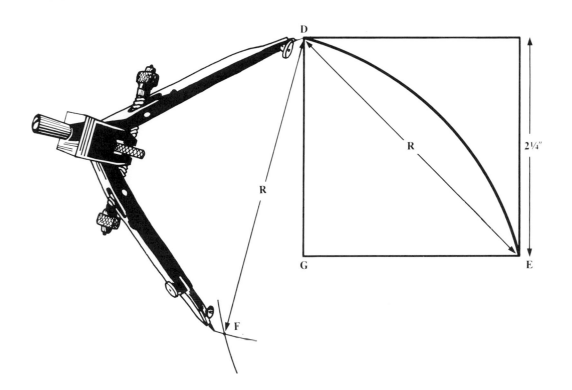

Fig. 29. *The radius (R) of the Curved Two-Patch arc is the diagonal of the square.*

2. *Place the pivot point of your compass on corner D.*

3. *Spread the compass until the pencil point crosses corner E. Do not change this setting for the following steps.*

4. *Without moving the pivot point from D, swing the compass pencil to the outside of corner G. Draw a short arc.*

5. *Move the pivot point of the compass to corner E and repeat the last step to cross the arc at point F.*

6. *Move the pivot point of the compass to the exact spot where the arcs cross at point F. With the compass pencil at corner D, swing an arc downward to E. This divides the square into concave and convex templates with 2¼" sides.*

To put it another way, the compass setting (or radius) for the arc is the diagonal of a given square. Drawing the small cross at point F establishes the focal point for the radius so you can bisect the square into convex and concave templates. (They do not include seam allowances.) Patches marked with these templates will be gently curved, but not as deep as quarter circles.

If you use the metric system, simply choose the number of centimeters you want your square to be. Then draw the arc by the method described above. I would suggest curved templates of five centimeters as a good basic pair.

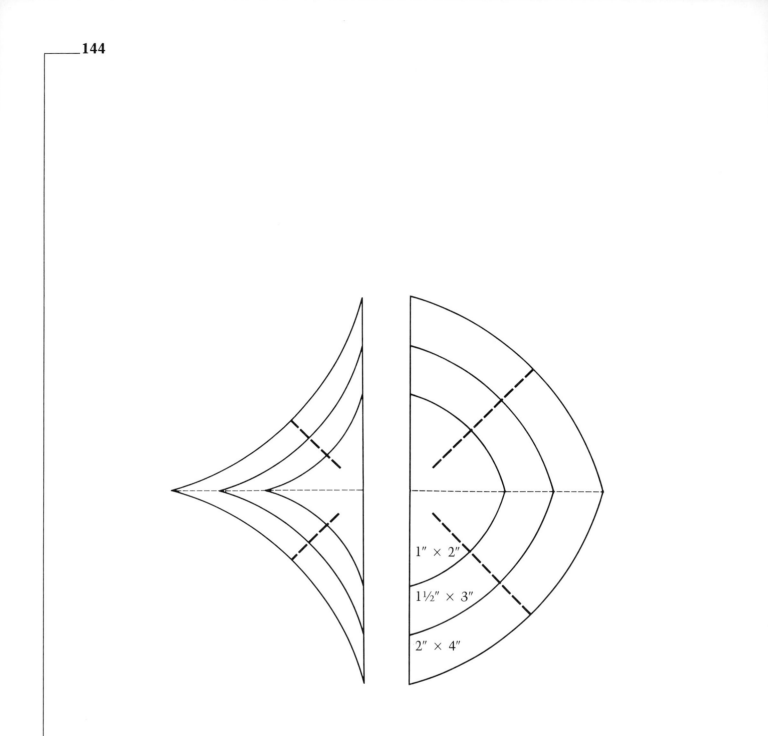

1″ × 2″

1½″ × 3″

2″ × 4″

Basic Curve Combinations

These combinations of the original templates, recognizable here as portions of a clamshell, occur often in the motifs where they are isolated peaks or domes. Use in designs based on 1″, 1½″ or 2″ units.

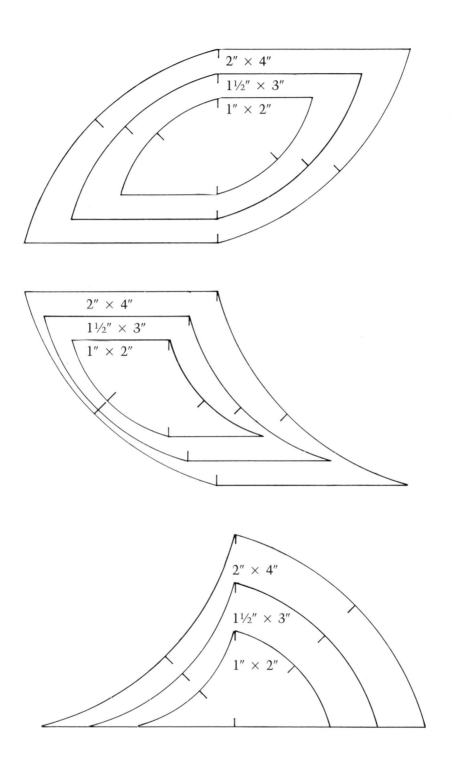

2″ × 4″
1½″ × 3″
1″ × 2″

2″ × 4″
1½″ × 3″
1″ × 2″

2″ × 4″
1½″ × 3″
1″ × 2″

More useful combinations of the original Curved Two-Patch templates for designs based on 1″, 1½″ or 2″ units.

Templates
for Elongated Curves

Starting on this page, there are six sets of templates for the elongated curves. Although these new curves appear in the motifs and short subjects in six different rectangles, the most common pair of elongated curves forms a rectangle of 1 x 2 units. The templates for this set are illustrated below. (These and the following templates do not include seam allowances.)

Notice that the smallest templates in the center of the illustration show dimensions based on a 1″ unit; the middle- sized ones are based on a 1½″ unit; the largest, on a 2″ unit. The sets of templates on the following pages are also "nested" and sized in the same manner. Except for the last one, each set is printed in three sizes. There are only two sizes for the elongated templates of 4 x 5 units (found only in *Curious Cat* and *Seaworthy*).

As an example of how to use the information printed below the templates, let's say you want to piece *Sunbonnet Sue, Herself* and have decided that each unit (one square of the grid in the working diagram) should be 2″. Notice that you need templates for elongated curves in a rectangle of 1 x 2 units. Now find the set of templates in this section that lists the same number of units (this page) and multiply by 2″. This tells you the templates must be 2″ x 4″, the largest pair in the set. By the same process, locate the other three sizes of elongated templates required for Sue.

If you work with the metric system, determine the size of the elongated curved templates by assigning centimeters to the basic unit. Multiply as above to discover what size of rectangle to draw. Then, to obtain templates for the elongated curves in centimeters, use one of the methods described in Section 1 for drawing the arc.

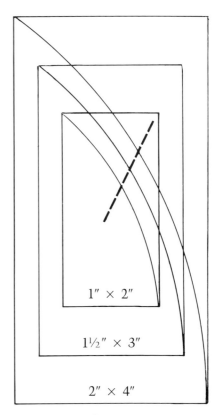

Templates of 1 × 2 units

Use in designs based on 1″, 1½″ or 2″ units.

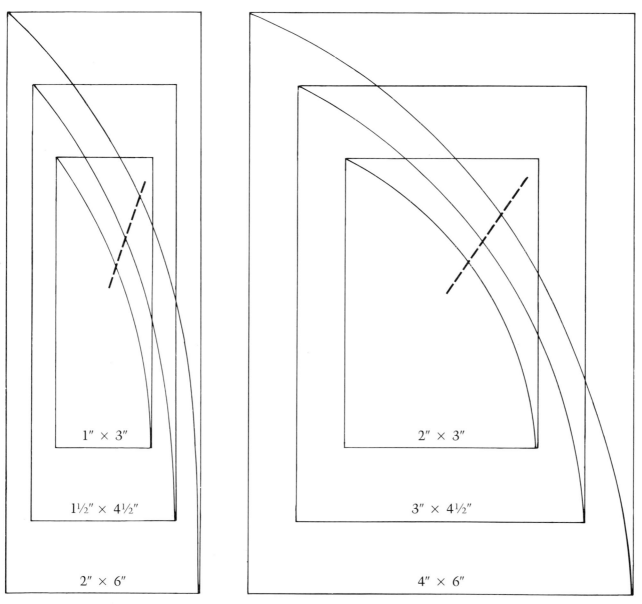

Templates of 1 × 3 units   *Templates of 2 × 3 units*

Use in designs based on 1″, 1½″ or 2″ units.

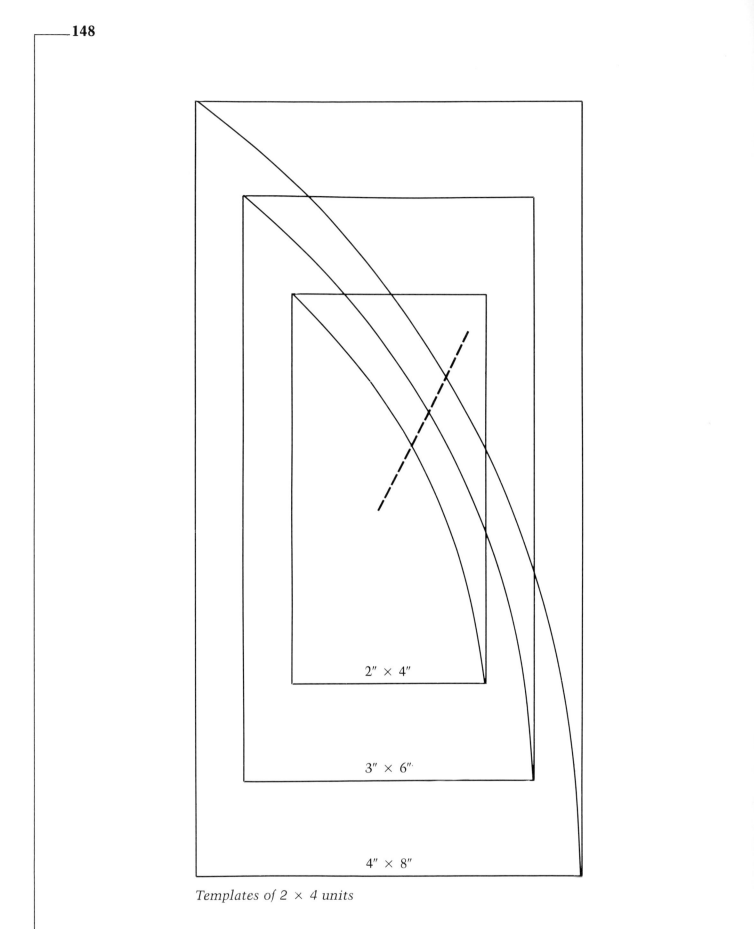

$2'' \times 4''$

$3'' \times 6''$

$4'' \times 8''$

Templates of 2 × 4 units

Use in designs based on 1″, 1½″ or 2″ units.

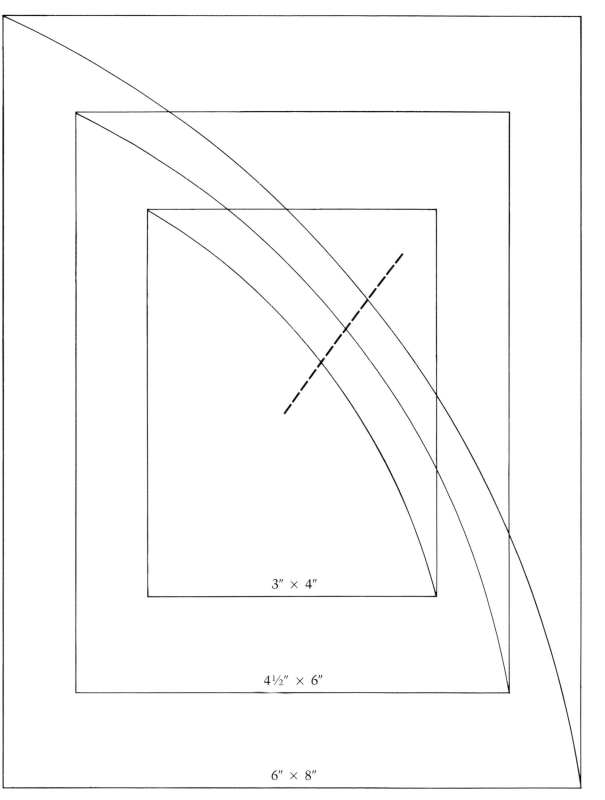

3″ × 4″

4½″ × 6″

6″ × 8″

Templates of 3 × 4 units

Use in designs based on 1″, 1½″ or 2″ units.

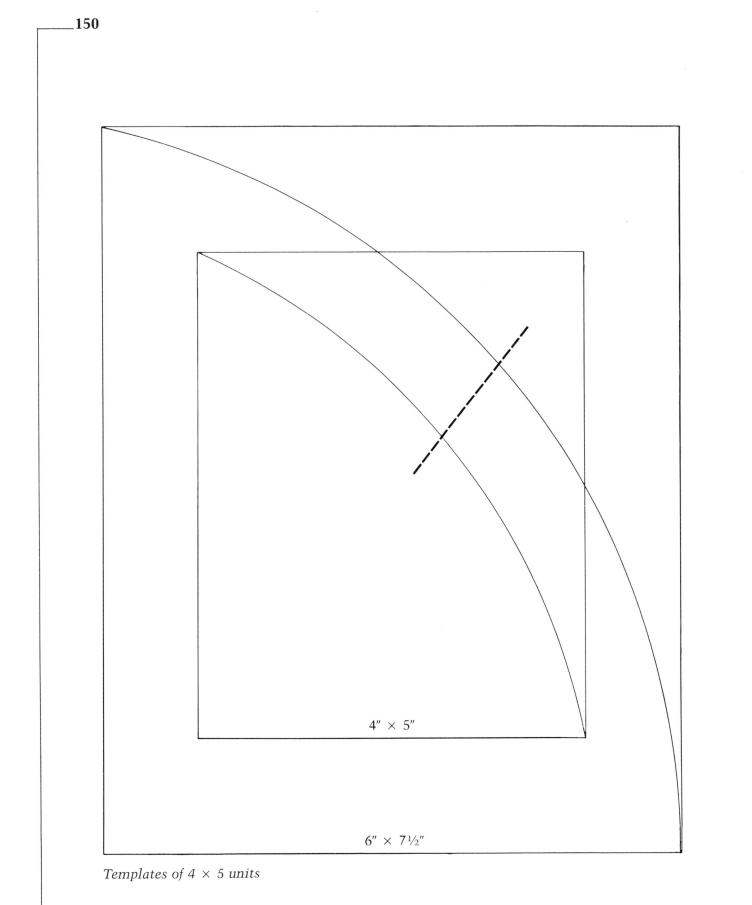

4″ × 5″

6″ × 7½″

Templates of 4 × 5 units

Use in designs based on 1″ and 1½″.

Some Applique Templates

*The appliques for **Cherry Blossom's** hair are above. The lower illustration is for her sandal, which can be pieced or appliqued. Add seam allowances to all.*

on fold

on
fold

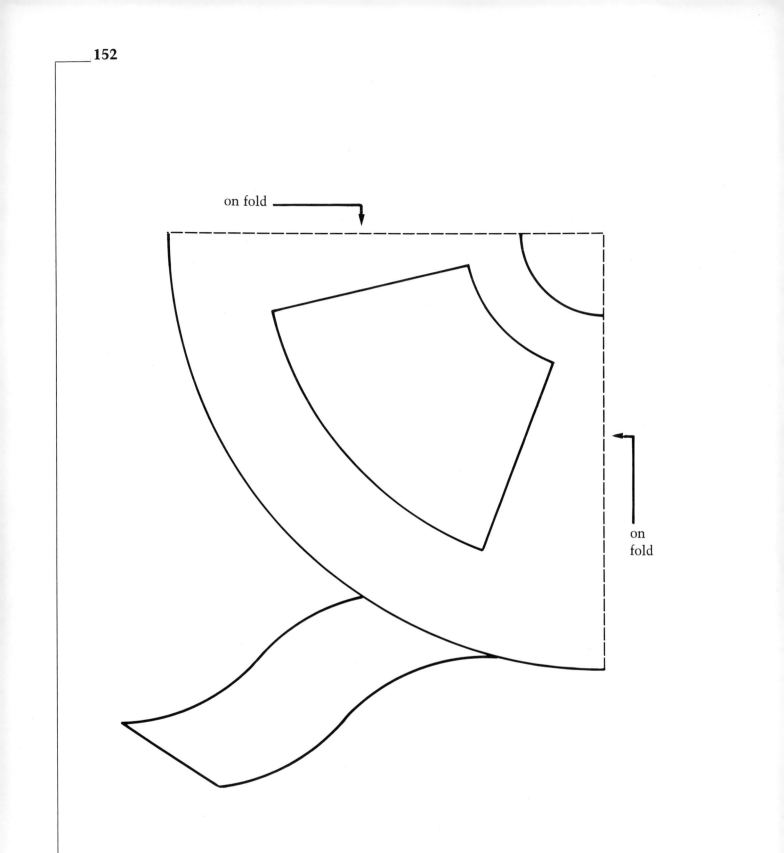

*Applique templates for **Reel One: Ted & Friends.***
One quarter of the reel and center hole are illustrated.
Add seam allowances.